MW01029579

SAT Vocabulary Flashcards
Extreme Flip-O-Matic
Third Edition

Other Kaplan Books for College-Bound Students

Test Preparation

SAT Vocabulary Words Flip-O-Matic, Third Edition
SAT Comprehensive 2007 Edition
SAT Premier 2007 Edition
SAT Critical Reading Workbook
SAT Math Workbook
SAT Writing Workbook
12 Practice Tests for the SAT

College Admissions and Financial Aid

101 Ways to Become the Perfect College Applicant
Hot Dates and Cold Pizza: A Compendium of Student Wisdom

SAT Vocabulary Flashcards
Extreme Flip-O-Matic
Third Edition

The Staff of Kaplan, Inc.

KAPLAN
PUBLISHING
New York • Chicago

Contributing Editor: Jon Zeitlin
Editorial Director: Jennifer Farthing
Editor: Eric Titner
Production Editor: Caitlin Ostrow
Production Artist: Virginia Byrne
Cover Designer: Carly Schnur

Published by Kaplan Publishing, a division of Kaplan, Inc.
888 Seventh Ave.
New York, NY 10106

Printed in the United States of America

December 2006
10 9 8 7 6 5 4 3 2 1

ISBN-13: 978-1-4195-5156-7
ISBN-10: 1-4195-5156-6

HOW TO USE THIS BOOK

More advanced than *Kaplan's SAT Vocabulary Words Flip-O-Matic*, *Kaplan's SAT Vocabulary Words Extreme Flip-O-Matic, Third Edition* is perfectly designed to help you learn 500 of the hardest essential SAT vocabulary words in a quick, easy, and fun way. Simply read the vocabulary word on the front of the flashcard and then flip to the back to see its definition, synonyms, and an example sentence with the SAT word in action. This amazing product conveniently allows you to skip over words once you've mastered them. All you have to do is clip or fold back the corner of the flashcard so that you can flip right by it on your next pass through the book. The *Extreme Flip-O-Matic, Third Edition* is packed with the toughest SAT vocabulary so you can flip your way to a higher score. Don't forget to flip the book over for the other half of the 500 hardest SAT words.

As a special bonus, we've included an SAT word root list at the back of this book for extra studying power. Grouping words together that share a common root meaning is a terrific and efficient way to familiarize yourself with strange or tough words you may encounter on the test.

Good luck, and happy flipping!

ABANDON

noun (uh baan duhn)

synonyms: breath, draft

The *zephyr* from the ocean made the intense heat on the beach bearable for the sunbathers.

a gentle breeze; something airy or unsubstantial

total lack of inhibition

With her strict parents out of town, Kelly danced all night with *abandon*.

synonyms: exuberance, enthusiasm

ZEPHYR

noun (z̄eh fuhr)

ABATE

verb (uh bayt)

the point of culmination; peak

The diva considered her appearance at the Metropolitan Opera to be the *zenith* of her career.

synonyms: acme, pinnacle

to decrease, to reduce

My hunger *abated* when I saw how filthy the chef's hands were.

synonyms: dwindle, ebb, recede

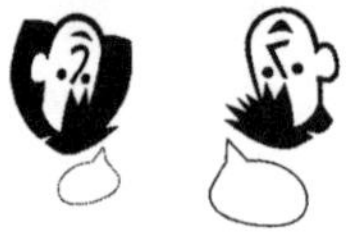

ZENITH

noun (zēē nihth)

ABET

verb (uh <u>beht</u>)

a strong desire, craving

Pregnant women commonly have a *yen* for pickles.

synonyms: thirst, yearning

to aid; to act as an accomplice

While Derwin robbed the bank, Marvin *abetted* his friend by pulling up the getaway car.

synonyms: help, succor, assist

YEN

noun (yehn)

ABJURE

verb (aab joor)

bent or twisted in shape or condition; dryly humorous

Every time she teased him, she shot her friends a *wry* smile.

synonyms: askew, sardonic

to renounce under oath; to abandon forever; to abstain from

> After having been devout for most of his life, he suddenly *abjured* his beliefs, much to his family's disappointment.

synonyms: renounce, disavow

WRY

adj (rie)

ABNEGATE

verb (<u>aab</u> nih gayt)

synonyms: beat, vanquish

The North *worsted* the South in America's Civil War.

to gain the advantage over; to defeat

to give up; to deny to oneself

After his retirement, the former police commissioner found it difficult to *abnegate* authority.

synonyms: abjure, surrender, renounce

WORST

verb (wuhrst)

ABORTIVE

adj (uh bohr tihv)

charming, happily engaging

Dawn gave the customs officers a *winsome* smile, and they let her pass without searching her bags.

synonyms: attractive, delightful

ending without results

Her *abortive* attempt to swim the full five miles left her frustrated.

synonyms: fruitless, futile, unsuccessful

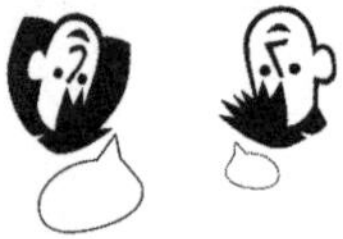

WINSOME

adj (wihn suhm)

ABROGATE

verb (aab ruh gayt)

clever; deceptive

Yet again, the *wily* coyote managed to elude the ranchers who wanted it captured.

synonyms: cunning, tricky, crafty

to annul; to abolish by authoritative action

The president's job is to *abrogate* any law that fosters inequality among citizens.

synonyms: nullify, revoke, repeal

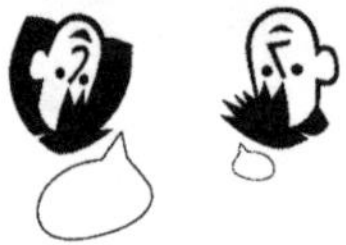

WILY

adj (wie lee)

ABSCOND

verb (aab <u>skahnd</u>)

to exercise authority or influence effectively

For such a young congressman, he *wielded* a lot of power.

synonyms: exert, handle

to leave quickly in secret

The criminal *absconded* during the night with all of his mother's money.

synonyms: slip, sneak, flee

WIELD

verb (weeld)

ABSTEMIOUS

adj (aab <u>stee</u> mee uhs)

to increase gradually; to begin to be

The moon was *waxing*, and would soon be full.

synonyms: enlarge, expand

done sparingly; consuming in moderation

> The spa served no sugar or wheat, but the clients found the retreat so calm that they didn't mind the *abstemious* rules.

synonyms: moderate, sparing, abstinent

WAX

verb (waaks)

ACCEDE

verb (aak <u>seed</u>)

undisciplined, unrestrained; reckless

The townspeople were outraged by the *wanton* display of disrespect when they discovered the statue of the town founder covered in graffiti.

synonyms: capricious, lewd, licentious

to express approval; to agree to

Once the mayor heard the reasonable request, she happily *acceded* to the proposal.

synonyms: consent, concur

WANTON

adj (wahn tuhn)

ACCLIVITY

noun (uh <u>klihv</u> ih tee)

sickly pale

The sick child had a *wan* face, in contrast to her rosy-cheeked sister.

synonyms: ashen, sickly

an incline or upward slope, the ascending side of a hill

> We were so tired from hiking the trail that by the time we reached the *acclivity*, it looked more like a mountain than a hill.

synonyms: ascent, upgrade

WAN

adj (wahn)

ACCRETION

noun (uh kree shuhn)

talkative, speaking easily, glib

The *voluble* man and his reserved wife proved the old saying that opposites attract.

synonyms: loquacious, verbose

a growth in size; an increase in amount

> The committee's strong fund-raising efforts resulted in an *accretion* of scholarship money.

synonyms: buildup, accumulation

VOLUBLE

adj (vahl yuh buhl)

a flight of missiles; round of gunshots

The troops fired a *volley* of bullets at the enemy, but they couldn't be sure how many hit their target.

synonyms: discharge, barrage

ACME

noun (aak mee)

the highest level or degree attainable

Just when he reached the *acme* of his power, the dictator was overthrown.

synonyms: apex, peak, summit

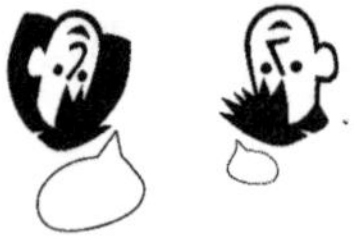

VOLLEY

noun (vah lee)

ACTUATE

verb (aak choo ayt)

loud, noisy

Amid the *vociferous* protests of the members of parliament, the prime minister continued his speech.

synonyms: vocal, boisterous

to put into motion, to activate; to motivate or influence to activity

The leaders rousing speech *actuated* the crowd into a peaceful protest.

synonyms: incite, instigate

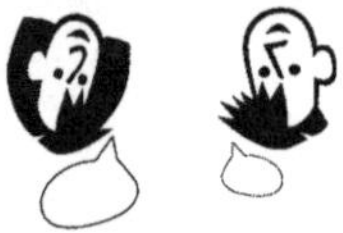

VOCIFEROUS

adj (voh sih fuhr uhs)

ACUITY

noun (uh kyoo ih tee)

to abuse verbally, berate

Vituperating someone is never a constructive way to effect change.

synonyms: scold, reproach, castigate

sharp vision or perception characterized by the ability to resolve fine detail

> With unusual *acuity*, she was able to determine that the photograph was out of focus.

synonyms: acuteness, sharpness

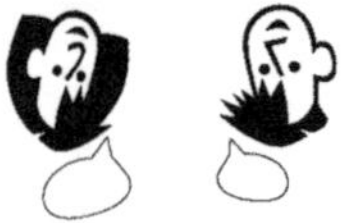

VITUPERATE

verb (vih too puhr ayt)

instinctive, not intellectual; deep, emotional

When my twin was wounded many miles away, I, too, had a *visceral* reaction.

synonyms: gut, earthy

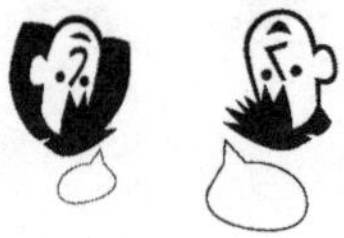

ACUMEN

noun (<u>aak</u> yuh muhn) (uh <u>kyoo</u> muhn)

sharpness of insight, mind, and understanding; shrewd judgment

The investor's financial *acumen* helped him to select high-yield stocks.

synonyms: discernment, shrewdness

VISCERAL

adj (vihs uhr uhl)

extremely poisonous; malignant; hateful

Alarmed at the *virulent* press he was receiving, the militant activist decided to go underground.

synonyms: infectious, toxic

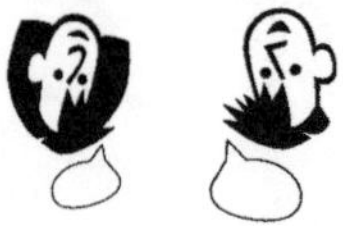

ADAMANT

adj (<u>aad</u> uh muhnt) (<u>aad</u> uh mihnt)

stubbornly unyielding

She was *adamant* about leaving the restaurant after the waiter was rude.

synonyms: inflexible, obdurate, inexorable

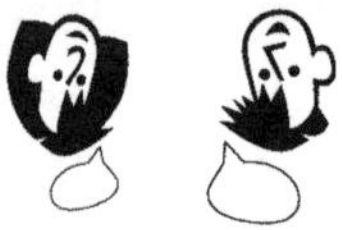

VIRULENT

adj (veer yuh luhnt)

ADEPT

adj (uh <u>dehpt</u>)

to clear of blame; support a claim

Tess felt *vindicated* when her prediction about the impending tornado came true.

synonyms: justify, exonerate

extremely skilled

She is *adept* at computing math problems in her head.

synonyms: quick, masterful

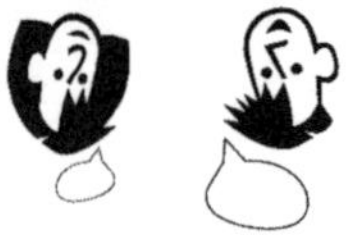

VINDICATE

verb (vihn dih kayt)

ADJUDICATE

verb (uh <u>jood</u> ih kayt)

vitality and energy

The *vim* with which she worked so early in the day explained why she was so productive.

synonyms: power, force

to hear and settle a matter; to act as a judge

The principal *adjudicated* the disagreement between two students.

synonyms: arbitrate, mediate

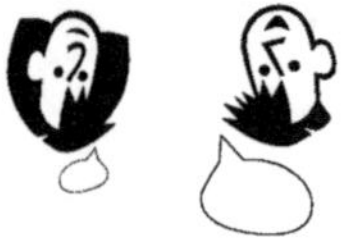

VIM

noun (vihm)

ADJURE

verb (uh joor)

to slander, defame

As gossip columnists often *vilify* celebrities, they're usually held in low regard.

synonyms: malign, slur

to appeal to

The criminal *adjured* to the court for mercy.

synonyms: beg, plead

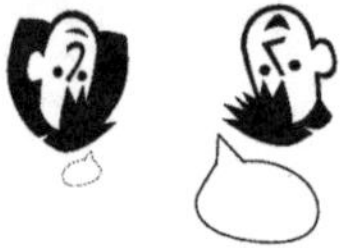

VILIFY

verb (vih lih fie)

ADMONISH

verb (aad <u>mahn</u> ihsh)

felt or undergone as if one were taking part in the experience or feelings of another

She lived *vicariously* through the characters in the adventure books she was always reading.

synonym: indirectly

to caution or warn gently in order to correct something

My mother *admonished* me about my poor grades.

synonyms: reprimand, rebuke

VICARIOUSLY

adverb (vie kaar ee uhs lee)

ADROIT

adj (uh droyt)

related to spring; fresh

Bea basked in the balmy *vernal* breezes, happy that winter was coming to an end.

synonyms: springlike, youthful

skillful; accomplished; highly competent

The *adroit* athlete completed even the most difficult obstacle course with ease.

synonyms: dexterous, proficient

VERNAL

adj (vuhr nuhl)

ADULATION

noun (aaj juh lay shuhn)

synonyms: dialect, lingo, jargon

Victor could not understand the *vernacular* of the south, where he had recently moved.

everyday language used by ordinary people; specialized language of a profession or region excessive flattery or admiration

> The *adulation* she showed her professor seemed insincere; I suspected she really wanted a better grade.

synonyms: fawning, buttering up

VERNACULAR

noun (vuhr naa kyoo luhr)

being without question, often used figuratively

My neighbor was a *veritable* goldmine of information when I was writing my term paper on the Civil Rights era because she had been a student organizer and protester.

synonyms: authentic, bona fide

ADUMBRATE

verb (aad uhm brayt) (uh duhm brayt)

to give a hint or indication of something to come

> Her constant complaining about the job *adumbrated* her intent to leave.

synonyms: foreshadow, suggest

VERITABLE

adj (vehr iht uh buhl)

AERIE

noun (ayr ee) (eer ee)

wordy

The DNA analyst's answer was so *verbose* that the jury had trouble grasping his point.

synonyms: loquacious, garrulous

a nest built high in the air; an elevated, often secluded, dwelling

Perched high among the trees, the eagle's *aerie* was filled with eggs.

synonyms: perch, stronghold

VERBOSE

adj (vuhr bohs)

AFFECTED

adj (uh <u>fehk</u> tihd)

accuracy; truth

She had a reputation for *veracity*, so everyone believed her version of the story.

synonyms: truthfulness, reliability

phony, artificial

> The *affected* hairdresser spouted French phrases, though she had never been to France.

synonyms: put-on, insincere, pretentious

VERACITY

noun (vuhr $\overline{aa}$ sih tee)

AGGREGATE

noun (aa grih giht)

marked by extreme intensity of emotions or convictions

She *vehemently* opposed the closing of the neighborhood garden, and was even arrested for protesting when the bulldozers came.

synonyms: vociferously, unequivocally

a collective mass, the sum total

> An *aggregate* of panic-stricken customers mobbed the bank, demanding their life savings.

synonyms: whole, entirety

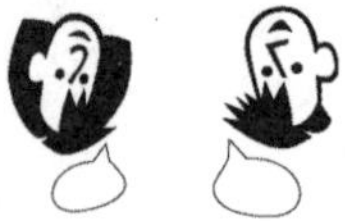

VEHEMENTLY

adverb (vee uh muhnt lee)

ALGORITHM

noun (<u>aal</u> guh rith uhm)

varied; marked with different colors

The *variegated* foliage of the jungle allows it to support thousands of animal species.

synonym: diversified

an established procedure for solving a problem or equation

The astronomer uses a series of *algorithms* to determine the path of the nearby comet.

synonym: calculation

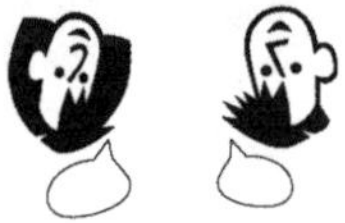

VARIEGATED

adj (vaar ee uh gayt ehd)

ALIMENTARY

adj (aal uh <u>mehn</u> tuh ree) (aal uh <u>mehn</u> tree)

the practice of lending money at exorbitant rates

The moneylender was convicted of *usury* when it was discovered that he charged 50 percent interest on all his loans.

synonyms: loan-sharking, interest

pertaining to food, nutrition, or digestion

> After a particularly good meal, Sherlock turned to his companion and exclaimed, “I feel quite good, very well fed. It was *alimentary* my dear Watson.”

synonyms: nourishing, nutritive

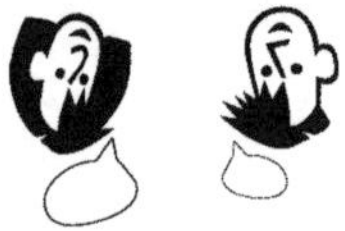

USURY

noun (yōō zhuh ree)

to dethrone, especially of priestly power

Any priest caught sullying the good name of his profession would certainly be *unfrocked.*

synonyms: demote, degrade

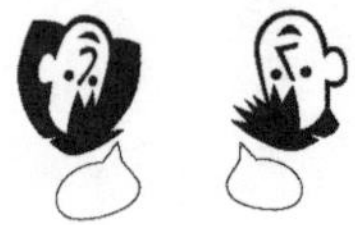

ALLAY

verb (uh lay)

to lessen, ease, reduce in intensity

Trying to *allay* their fears, the nurse sat with them all night.

synonyms: alleviate, soothe

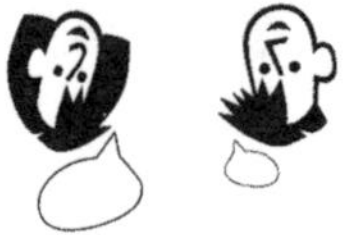

UNFROCK

verb (uhn frahk)

AMITY

noun (aa mih tee)

synonyms: dishonorable, indefensible

unconscionable.

After she promised me the project, the fact that she gave it to someone else is

unscrupulous; shockingly unfair or unjust

friendship, good will

Correspondence over the years contributed to a lasting *amity* between the women.

synonyms: harmony, benevolence

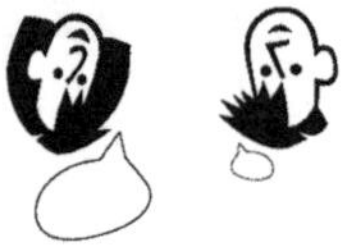

UNCONSCIONABLE

adj (uhn kahn shuhn uh buhl)

AMORPHOUS

adj (<u>ay</u> <u>mohr</u> fuhs)

synonyms: weird, eerie

Though they weren't related, their resemblance was *uncanny*.

so keen and perceptive as to seem supernatural, peculiarly unsettling having no definite form

The Blob featured an *amorphous* creature that was constantly changing shape.

synonyms: shapeless, indistinct

UNCANNY

adj (uhn kaa nee)

ANIMUS

noun (aan uh muhs)

synonym: supervision

Under the *tutelage* of her older sister, the young orphan was able to persevere.

guardianship, guidance

a feeling of animosity or ill will

Though her teacher had failed her, she displayed no *animus* toward him.

synonyms: hostility, animosity

TUTELAGE

noun (toot uh lihj)

ANODYNE

noun (<u>aan</u> uh dyen)

swollen as from a fluid, bloated

In the process of osmosis, water passes through the walls of *turgid* cells, ensuring that they never contain too much water.

synonym: distended

a source of comfort; a medicine that relieves pain

> The sound of classical music is usually just the *anodyne* I need after a tough day at work.

synonyms: analgesic, painkiller

TURGID

adj (tuhr jihd)

disposed to fight, belligerent

The bully was initially *truculent* but eventually stopped picking fights at the least provocation.

synonyms: antagonistic, combative

ANOMALY

noun (uh <u>nahm</u> uh lee)

a deviation from the common rule, something that is difficult to classify

Among the top-ten albums of the year was one *anomaly*—a compilation of polka classics.

synonym: irregularity

TRUCULENT

adj (truhk yuh lehnt)

ANTHROPOMORPHIC

adj (aan thruh poh mohr fihk)

to beat severely, defeat

The inexperienced young boxer was *trounced* in a matter of minutes.

synonyms: vanquish, conquer

suggesting human characteristics for animals and inanimate things

> Many children's stories feature *anthropomorphic* animals such as talking wolves and pigs.

synonym: humanlike

TROUNCE
verb (trowns)

ANTIQUATED

adj (<u>aan</u> tih kway tihd)

trembling, timid; easily shaken

The *tremulous* kitten had been separated from her mother.

synonyms: shaking, timorous, anxious

too old to be fashionable or useful

Next to her coworker's brand-new model, Marisa's computer looked *antiquated*.

synonyms: outdated, obsolete

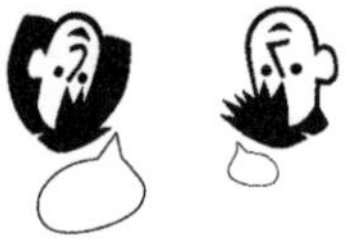

TREMULOUS

adj (treh myoo luhs)

APHORISM

noun (<u>aa</u> fuhr ihz uhm)

short-lived, existing only briefly

The actress' popularity proved *transitory* when her play folded within the month.

synonyms: transient, ephemeral, momentary

a short statement of a principle

The country doctor was given to such *aphorisms* as “Still waters run deep.”

synonyms: adage, proverb

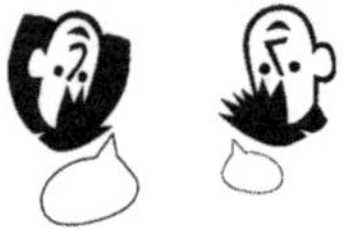

TRANSITORY

adj (traan sih tohr ee)

APLOMB

noun (uh plahm) (uh pluhm)

passing with time, temporary; short-lived

The reporter lived a *transient* life, staying in one place only long enough to cover the current story.

synonyms: brief, transitory

self-confident assurance; poise

> For such a young dancer, she had great *aplomb*, making her perfect to play the young princess.

synonyms: coolness, composure

TRANSIENT

adj (traan see uhnt)

APOSTATE

noun (uh pahs tayt)

the path followed by a moving object, whether through space or otherwise; flight

The *trajectory* of the pitched ball was interrupted by an unexpected bird.

synonyms: path, route, course

one who renounces a religious faith

So that he could divorce his wife, the king scoffed at the church doctrines and declared himself an *apostate*.

synonyms: traitor, defector, deserter

TRAJECTORY

noun (truh jehk tuh ree)

APPOSITE

adj (aap puh ziht)

to praise or publicize loudly or extravagantly

She *touted* her skills as superior to ours, though in fact, we were all at the same level.

synonyms: acclaim, proclaim

strikingly appropriate or well adapted

> The lawyer presented an *apposite* argument upon cross-examining the star witness.

synonyms: apt, relevant, suitable

TOUT

verb (towt)

having many twists and turns; highly complex

To reach the remote inn, the travelers had to negotiate a *tortuous* path.

synonyms: winding, circuitous

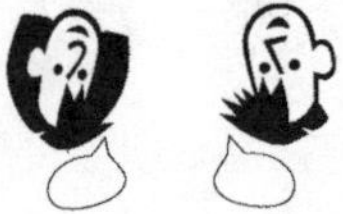

APPRISE

verb (uh <u>priez</u>)

to give notice to, inform

> "Thanks for *apprising* me that the test time has been changed," said Emanuel.

synonym: notify

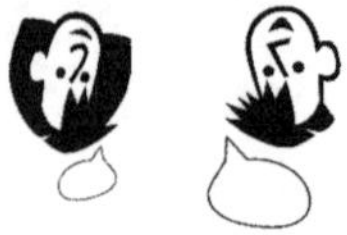

TORTUOUS

adj (tohr choo uhs)

one who flatters in the hope of gaining favors

The king was surrounded by *toadies* who rushed to agree with whatever outrageous thing he said.

synonyms: sycophant, parasite

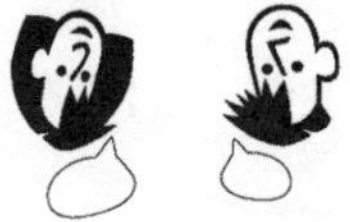

APPROPRIATE

verb (uh <u>proh</u> pree ayt)

to assign to a particular purpose, allocate

The mayor *appropriated* funds for the clean-up effort.

synonyms: appoint, earmark

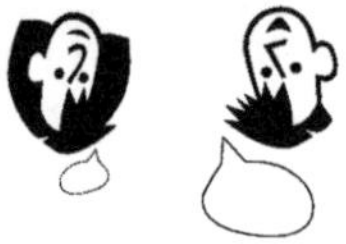

TOADY

noun (tōh dee)

ARABLE

adj (aa ruh buhl)

existing in title only; having a title without the functions or responsibilities

His prestige was merely a result of his *titular* rank, as he had no real power.

synonyms: honorary, named

suitable for cultivation

The overpopulated country desperately needed more *arable* land.

synonyms: farmable, fertile

TITULAR

adj (tihch yoo luhr)

ARCANE

adj (ahr kayn)

to block or prevent from happening; frustrate, defeat the hopes or aspirations of

Thwarted in its attempt to get at the bananas inside the box, the chimp began to squeal.

synonyms: oppose, foil, frustrate

secret, obscure; known only to a few

The *arcane* rituals of the sect were passed down through many generations.

synonyms: esoteric, mysterious

THWART

verb (thwahrt)

ARCHIPELAGO

noun (ahr kuh <u>pehl</u> uh goh)

concise, brief, free of extra words

Her *terse* style of writing was widely praised by the editors, who had been used to seeing long-winded material.

synonyms: succinct, brusque

a large group of islands

Between villages in the Stockholm *archipelago*, boat taxis are the only form of transportation.

synonyms: cluster, scattering

TERSE

adj (tuhrs)

ARREARS

noun (uh <u>reerz</u>)

having little substance or strength; flimsy, weak

Francine's already *tenuous* connection to her cousins was broken when they moved away and left no forwarding address.

synonyms: thin, shaky

unpaid, overdue debts or bills; neglected obligations

After the expensive lawsuit, Dominic's accounts were in *arrears*.

synonym: balance due

TENUOUS

adj (tehn yoo uhs)

ARROGATE

verb (aa ruh gayt)

synonym: canon

One of the *tenets* of Islam is that it is not acceptable to eat pork.

a principle, belief, or doctrine accepted by members of a group to claim without justification; to claim for oneself without right

> Lynn watched in astonishment as her boss *arrogated* the credit for her brilliant work on the project.

synonyms: take, presume, appropriate

TENET

noun (teh niht)

tending to persist or cling; persistent in adhering to something valued or habitual

For years, against all odds, women *tenaciously* fought for the right to vote.

synonyms: stubborn, dogged, obstinate

ASKANCE

adv (uh skaans)

with disapproval; with a skeptical sideways glance

> She looked *askance* at her son's failing report card as he mumbled that he had done all the schoolwork.

synonym: suspiciously

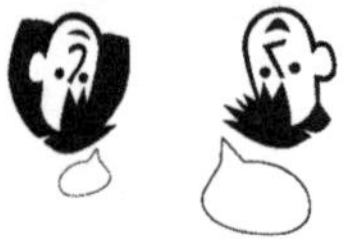

TENACIOUS

adj (tuh nay shuhs)

having to do with, or limited by time

The story lacked a sense of the *temporal*, so we couldn't figure out if the events took place in one evening or over the course of a year.

synonyms: chronological, passing, ephemeral

ASSENT

verb (uh <u>sehnt</u>)

to agree, as to a proposal

After careful deliberation, the CEO *assented* to the proposed merger.

synonyms: accede, yield, concur

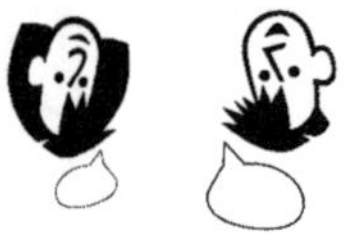

TEMPORAL

adj (tehm puhr uhl) (tehm pruhl)

ATAVISTIC

adj (aat uh <u>vihs</u> tik)

stormy, turbulent

Our camping trip was cut short when the sun shower we were expecting turned into a *tempestuous* downpour.

synonyms: tumultuous, blustery

characteristic of a former era, ancient

After spending three weeks on a desert island, Roger became a survivalist with *atavistic* skills that helped him endure.

synonyms: old-fashioned, outdated

TEMPESTUOUS

adj (tehm pehs choo uhs)

unreasonable or foolhardy disregard for danger, recklessness

I offered her a ride since it was late at night, but she had the *temerity* to say she'd rather walk.

synonym: boldness

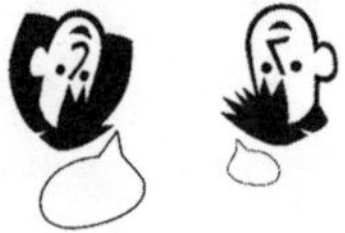

AUTOCRAT

noun (<u>aw</u> toh kraat)

a dictator

Mussolini has been described as an *autocrat* who tolerated no opposition.

synonyms: tyrant, despot

TEMERITY

noun (teh mehr ih tee)

AVER

verb (uh vuhr)

gaudy, cheap, showy

The performer changed into her *tawdry* costume and stepped onto the stage.

synonyms: flashy, chintzy

to declare to be true, to affirm

"Yes, he was holding a gun," the witness *averred*.

synonyms: assert, attest

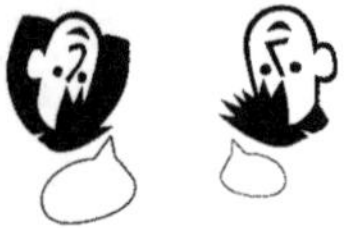

TAWDRY

adj (taw dree)

AVUNCULAR

adj (ah <u>vuhng</u> kyuh luhr)

having to do with needless repetition, redundancy

I know he was only trying to clarify things, but his *tautological* statements confused me even more.

synonyms: verbose, wordy

like an uncle in behavior, especially in kindness and warmth

The coach's *avuncular* style made him well-liked.

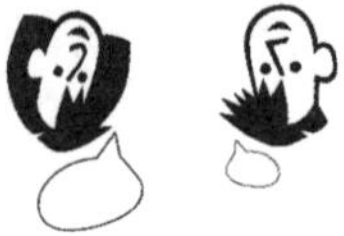

TAUTOLOGICAL

adj (tawt uh lah jih kuhl)

AWRY

adv (uh <u>rie</u>)

equal in value or effect

If she didn't get concert tickets to see her favorite band, it would be *tantamount* to a tragedy.

synonyms: parallel, synonymous, equivalent

crooked, askew, amiss

> Something must have gone *awry* in the computer system because some of my files are missing.

synonyms: aslant, wrong

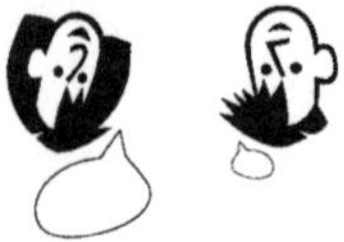

TANTAMOUNT

adj (taan tuh mownt)

BALK

verb (bawk)

producing a sensation of touch

The Museum of Natural History displays objects for people to touch so that they have a *tactile* understanding of how different plants and animals lived.

synonyms: perceptible, tangible

to stop short and refuse to go on

When the horse *balked* at jumping over the high fence, the rider was thrown off.

synonyms: flinch, shirk from

TACTILE

adj (taak tuhl) (taak tiel)

BALLAST

noun (<u>baal</u> uhst)

a person devoted to pleasure and luxury

A confirmed *sybarite*, the nobleman fainted at the thought of having to leave his palace and live in a small cottage.

synonyms: sensualist, voluptuary

a structure that helps to stabilize or steady

Communication and honesty are the true *ballasts* of a good relationship.

synonyms: counterweight, balancer

SYBARITE

noun (sih buh riet)

BEATIFIC

adj (bee uh <u>tihf</u> ihk)

to conquer, overcome

The blind woman *surmounted* great obstacles to become a well-known trial lawyer.

synonyms: clear, hurdle, leap

displaying calmness and joy, relating to a state of celestial happiness

After spending three months in India, she had a *beatific* peace about her.

synonyms: angelic, blissful

SURMOUNT

verb (suhr mownt)

BECALM

verb (bih kahm)

to replace (another) by force, to take the place of

The overthrow of the government meant finding a new leader to *supplant* the tyrannical former one.

synonyms: displace, supersede

to stop the progress of, to soothe

The warm air *becalmed* the choppy waves.

synonyms: quiet, allay, still

SUPPLANT

verb (suh plant)

to cause to be set aside; to force out of use as inferior, replace

Her computer was still running version 2.0 of the software, which had long since been *superseded* by at least three more versions.

synonyms: supplant, displace

BECLOUD

verb (bih klowd)

to make less visible, obscure, or blur

> Her ambivalence about the long commute *beclouded* her enthusiasm about the job.

synonyms: muddle, cloud

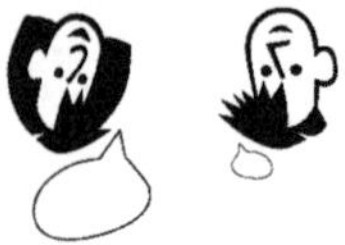

SUPERSEDE

verb (soo puhr seed)

extra, more than necessary

The extra recommendations Jake included in his application were *superfluous*, as only one was required.

synonyms: excess, surplus

BEDRAGGLED

adj (bih draag uhld)

soiled, wet and limp; dilapidated

The child's *bedraggled* blanket needed a good cleaning.

synonyms: dishevelled, disordered, threadbare

SUPERFLUOUS

adj (soo puhr floo uhs)

to tarnish, taint

With the help of a public-relations firm, he was able to restore his *sullied* reputation.

synonyms: defile, besmirch

BEGET

verb (bih geht)

to produce, especially as an effect or outgrowth; to bring about

> The mayor believed that finding petty offenders would help reduce serious crime because, he argued, small crimes *beget* big crimes.

synonym: cause, breed

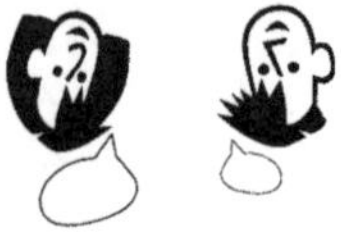

SULLY

verb (suh lee)

BEHEMOTH

noun (buh hee muhth)

hidden, secret; underground

Subterranean tracks were created for the trains after it was decided they had run out of room above ground.

synonyms: buried, concealed, sunken

something of monstrous size or power; huge creature

> The budget became such a *behemoth* that observers believed the film would never make a profit.

synonyms: giant, mammoth

SUBTERRANEAN

adj (suhb tuh ray nee uhn)

BENEFICENT

adj (buh <u>nehf</u> ih suhnt)

synonyms: stump, baffle, foil

The police effort to capture the bank robber was *stymied* when he escaped through a rear window.

to block or thwart

pertaining to an act of kindness

The *beneficent* man donated the money anonymously.

synonyms: charitable, generous

STYMIE
verb (stie mee)

BERATE

verb (bih rayt)

imposing severe, rigorous standards

Many people found it difficult to live up to the *stringent* moral standards imposed by the Puritans.

synonyms: restricted, tight, demanding

to scold harshly

When my manager found out I had handled the situation so insensitively, he *berated* me.

synonyms: criticize, scold

STRINGENT

adj (strihn guhnt)

BILIOUS

adj (<u>bihl</u> yuhs)

loud, harsh, unpleasantly noisy

The traveler's *strident* manner annoyed the flight attendant, but she managed to keep her cool.

synonyms: grating, shrill, discordant

ill-tempered; sickly, ailing

The party ended early when the *bilious* 5-year-old tried to run off with the birthday girl's presents.

synonyms: pale, feeble, peevish

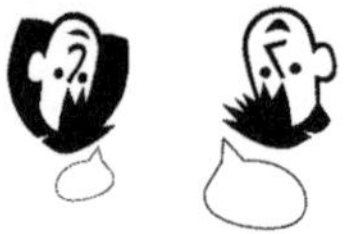

STRIDENT

adj (strie dehnt)

BLASPHEMOUS

adj (<u>blaas</u> fuh muhs)

to arrange or divide into layers

Schliemann *stratified* the numerous layers of Troy, an archeological dig that remains legendary.

synonyms: grade, separate

cursing, profane; extremely irreverent

The politician's offhanded biblical references seemed *blasphemous*, given the context of the orderly meeting.

synonyms: impious, profane, sacrilegious

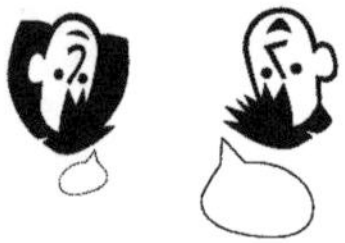

STRATIFY

verb (straa tuh fie)

to specify as a condition or requirement of an agreement or offer

The contract *stipulated* that if the movie was never filmed, the actress got paid anyway.

synonyms: specifize, detail, designate

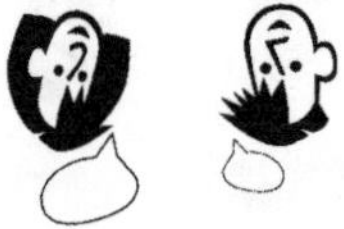

BLATANT

adj (<u>blay</u> tnt)

completely obvious and conspicuous, especially in an offensive, crass manner

> Such *blatant* advertising within the bounds of the school drew protest from parents.

synonyms: obvious, flagrant

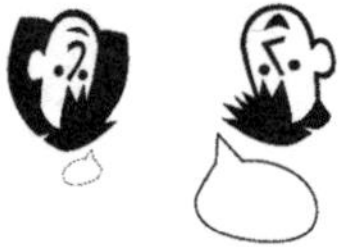

STIPULATE

verb (st<u>ihp</u> yuh layt)

to be sparing or frugal; to restrict with respect to a share or allowance

Don't *stint* on the mayonnaise, because I don't like my sandwich too dry.

synonyms: skimp, scrimp

BLITHELY

adv (<u>blieth</u> lee)

merrily, lightheartedly cheerful; without appropriate thought

> Wanting to redecorate the office, she *blithely* assumed her co-workers wouldn't mind and moved the furniture in the space.

synonym: in a carefree manner

STINT

verb (stihnt)

BOMBASTIC

adj (bahm baast ihk)

a state of static balance or equilibrium; stagnation

The rusty, ivy-covered World War II tank had obviously been in *stasis* for years.

synonyms: inertia, standstill

high-sounding but meaningless; ostentatiously lofty in style

> Mussolini's speeches were mostly *bombastic*; his outrageous claims had no basis in fact.

synonyms: grandiose, inflated

STASIS

noun (stay sihs)

marked by outstanding strength and vigor of body, mind, or spirit

The 85-year old went to the market every day, impressing her neighbors with her *stalwart* routine.

synonyms: strong, bold

BOVINE

adj (boh vien)

relating to cows; having qualities characteristic of a cow, such as sluggishness or dullness

His *bovine* demeanor did nothing to engage me.

synonyms: dull, placid

STALWART

adj (stahl wuhrt)

BRAGGART

noun (braag uhrt)

filthy and degraded as the result of neglect or poverty

The *squalid* living conditions in the building outraged the new tenants.

synonyms: unclean, foul

a person who brags or boasts in a loud and empty manner

> Usually the biggest *braggart* at the company party, Susan's boss was unusually quiet at this year's event.

synonyms: boaster, showoff

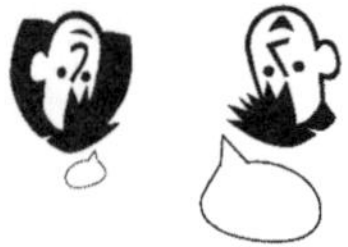

SQUALID

adj (skwa lihd)

BROACH

verb (brohch)

frolicsome, playful

The lakeside vacation meant more *sportive* opportunities for the kids than the wine tour through France.

synonyms: frisky, merry

to mention or suggest for the first time

> Sandy wanted to go to college away from home, but he didn't know how to *broach* the topic with his parents.

synonyms: introduce, propose

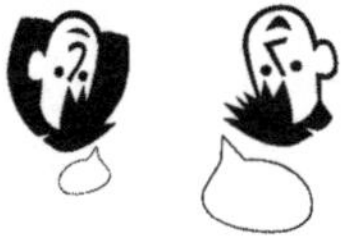

SPORTIVE

adj (spohr tihv)

BUCOLIC

adj (byoo kahl lihk)

having the ring of truth but actually being untrue; deceptively attractive

After I followed up with some research on the matter, I realized that the charismatic politician's argument had been *specious.*

synonyms: misleading, untrue, captious

pastoral, rural

My aunt likes the hustle and bustle of the city, but my uncle prefers a more *bucolic* setting.

synonyms: rustic, country

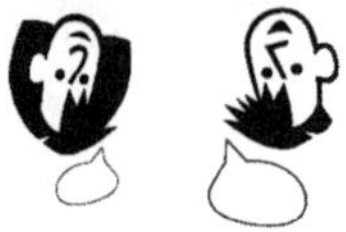

SPECIOUS

adj (spee shuhs)

BURNISH

verb (<u>buhr</u> nihsh)

synonyms: restrained, simple

When he was in training, the athlete preferred to live in a *spartan* room, so he could shut out all distractions.

highly self-disciplined; frugal, austere

to polish; to make smooth and bright

Mr. Frumpkin loved to stand in the sun and *burnish* his luxury car.

synonyms: shine, buff

SPARTAN

adj (spahr tihn)

BURSAR

noun (buhr suhr) (buhr sahr)

exhibiting great immaturity and lack of judgment

After Sean's *sophomoric* behavior, he was grounded for weeks.

synonyms: juvenile, immature

treasurer or keeper of funds

The *bursar* of the school was in charge of allocating all scholarship funds.

SOPHOMORIC

adj (sahf mohr ihk)

CACHE

noun (caash)

anxious, concerned; full of desire, eager

Overjoyed to see the pop idol in her very presence, the *solicitous* store owner stood ready to serve.

synonyms: considerate, careful

a hiding place; stockpile

It's good to have a *cache* where you can stash your cash.

synonyms: hoard, reserve

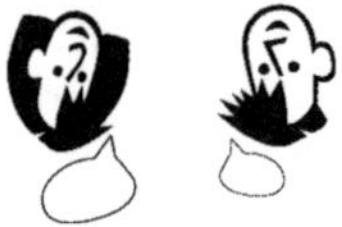

SOLICITOUS

adj (suh lih sih tuhs)

CACOPHONY

noun (kuh <u>kah</u> fuh nee)

a temporary stay, visit

After graduating from college, Iliani embarked on a *sojourn* to China.

synonyms: layover, stay, rest

a jarring, unpleasant noise

As I walked into the open-air market after my nap, a *cacophony* of sounds surrounded me.

synonyms: clatter, racket

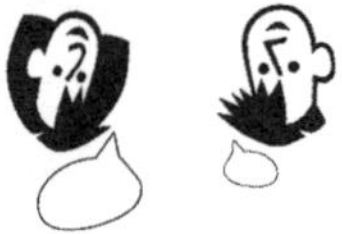

SOJOURN

noun (soh juhrn)

CALUMNY

noun (<u>kaa</u> luhm nee)

a nickname

One of former president Ronald Reagan's *sobriquets* was *The Gipper.*

synonyms: alias, pseudonym

a false and malicious accusation; misrepresentation

The unscrupulous politician used *calumny* to bring down his opponent in the senatorial race.

synonyms: libel, defamation, slander

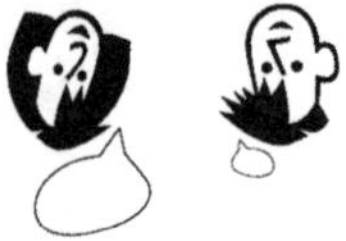

SOBRIQUET

noun (sōh brih kay) (sōh brih keht)

CANTANKEROUS

adj (kaan <u>taang</u> kuhr uhs)

a well-paying job or office that requires little or no work

The corrupt mayor made sure to set up all his relatives in *sinecures* within the administration.

having a difficult, uncooperative, or stubborn disposition

> The most outwardly *cantankerous* man in the nursing home was surprisingly sweet and loving with his grandchildren.

synonyms: contentious, ornery

SINECURE

noun (sien ih kyoor)

CAPTIOUS

adj (<u>kaap</u> shuhs)

apelike; relating to apes

Early man was more *simian* in appearance than is modern man.

synonyms: anthropoid, primate

marked by the tendency to point out trivial faults; intended to confuse in an argument

I resent the way he asked that *captious* question.

synonyms: critical, censorious

SIMIAN

adj (sih mee uhn)

CATACLYSMIC

adj (kaat uh klihz mihk)

angelic, sweet

Selena's *seraphic* appearance belied her nasty, bitter personality.

synonyms: heavenly, cherubic

severely destructive

By all appearances, the storm seemed *cataclysmic*, though it lasted only a short while.

synonyms: catastrophic, tragic

SERAPHIC

adj (seh rah fihk)

CATALYST

noun (<u>kaat</u> uhl ihst)

to set apart, seclude

When juries are *sequestered*, it can take days, even weeks, to come up with a verdict.

synonyms: segregate, isolate

something that provokes or speeds up significant change, especially without being affected by the consequences

> Technology has been a *catalyst* for the expansion of alternative education, such as home schooling and online courses.

synonym: accelerator

SEQUESTER

verb (suh kweh stuhr)

CAUCUS

noun (<u>kaw</u> kuhs)

influential in an original way, providing a basis for further development; creative

The scientist's discovery proved to be *seminal* in the area of quantum physics.

synonyms: original, generative

a closed committee within a political party; a private committee meeting

The president met with the delegated *caucus* to discuss the national crisis.

synonyms: assembly, convention

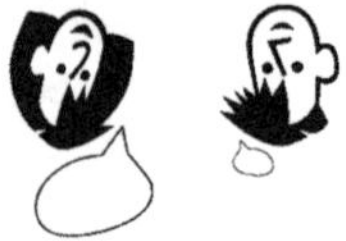

SEMINAL

adj (seh muhn uhl)

CAUSTIC

adj (<u>kah</u> stihk)

behavior that promotes rebellion or civil disorder against the state

Li was arrested for *sedition* after he gave a fiery speech in the main square.

synonyms: insurrection, conspiracy

biting, sarcastic

Writer Dorothy Parker gained her reputation for *caustic* wit, and her tombstone is inscribed with a fittingly clever “Excuse my dust.”

synonyms: sardonic, incisive

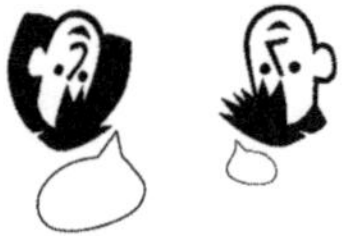

SEDITION

noun (seh dih shuhn)

CEDE

verb (seed)

not specifically pertaining to religion, relating to the world

Although his favorite book was the Bible, the archbishop also read *secular* works such as mysteries.

synonyms: temporal, material

to surrender possession of something

Argentina *ceded* the Falkland Islands to Britain after a brief war.

synonyms: resign, yield, relinquish

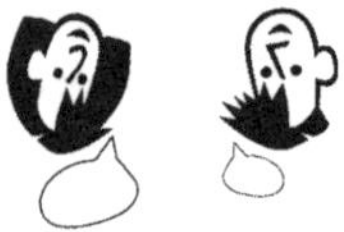

SECULAR

adj (seh kyuh luhr)

CELERITY

noun (seh leh rih tee)

morally degraded, unpleasant

The tour guide avoided the *seamy* parts of town.

synonyms: sordid, sleazy

speed, haste

The celebrity ran past his fans with great *celerity*.

synonyms: swiftness, briskness

SEAMY

adj (see mee)

CENSORIOUS

adj (sehn <u>sohr</u> ee uhs)

synonyms: painstaking, meticulous

After the storm had destroyed their antique lamp, the Millers worked to repair it with *scrupulous* care.

acting in strict regard for what is considered proper; punctiliously exact critical; tending to blame and condemn

Closed-minded people tend to be *censorious* of others.

synonym: fault-finding

SCRUPULOUS

adj (skroop yuh luhs)

CERTITUDE

noun (suhr tih tood)

synonym: scholar

The *savant* so impressed us with his knowledge that we asked him to come speak at our school.

a person of learning; especially one with knowledge in a special field assurance, freedom from doubt

The witness' *certitude* about the night in question had a big impact on the jury.

synonyms: certainty, conviction

SAVANT

noun (suh vahnt)

CESSATION

noun (seh <u>say</u> shuhn)

cold and steady in mood, gloomy; slow to act

Her *saturnine* expression every day made her hard to be around.

synonyms: sullen, bitter

a temporary or complete halt

The *cessation* of hostilities ensured that soldiers were able to spend the holidays with their families.

synonyms: arrest, termination

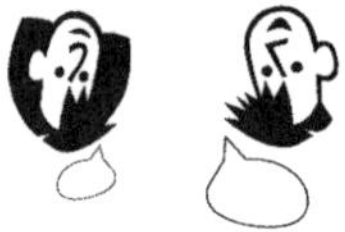

SATURNINE

adj (saat uhr nien)

to satisfy (as a need or desire) fully or to excess

After years of journeying around the world with nothing but backpacks, the friends had finally *satiated* their desire to travel.

synonym: gorge

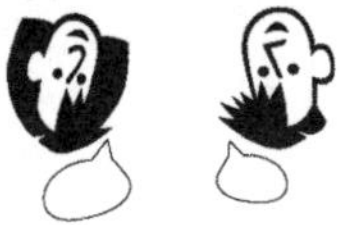

CHARY

adj (<u>chahr</u> ee)

watchful, cautious; extremely shy

Mindful of the fate of the Titanic, the captain was *chary* of navigating the iceberg-filled sea.

synonyms: wary, careful

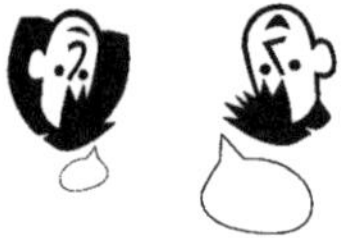

SATIATE

verb (say shee ayt)

hypocritically devout; acting morally superior to another

The *sanctimonious* columnist turned out to have been hiding a gambling problem that cost his family everything.

synonyms: pious, self-righteous

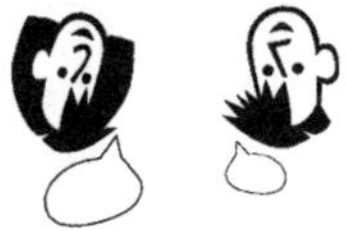

CHIMERICAL

adj (kie mehr ih kuhl) (kie meer ih kuhl)

fanciful; imaginary, impossible

The inventor's plans seemed *chimerical* to the conservative businessman from whom he was asking for financial support.

synonyms: illusory, unreal

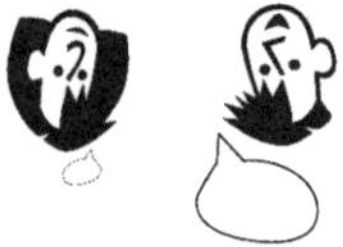

SANCTIMONIOUS

adj (saangk tih moh nee uhs)

CIRCUITOUS

adj (suhr kyoo ih tuhs)

prominent, of notable significance

His most *salient* characteristic is his tendency to dominate every conversation.

synonyms: noticeable, marked, outstanding

indirect, roundabout

> The venue was only a short walk from the train station, but a roadblock meant I had to take a *circuitous* route.

synonyms: lengthy, devious

SALIENT

adj (say lee uhnt)

CIRCUMVENT

verb (suhr kuhm vehnt)

synonym: lustful

His television character was wholesomely funny, so audiences who saw his stand-up comedy routine were shocked by how *salacious* his jokes were.

appealing to sexual desire

to go around; avoid

Laura was able to *circumvent* the hospital's regulations, slipping into her mother's room long after visiting hours were over.

synonyms: evade, sidestep

SALACIOUS

adj (suh lay shuhs)

CLOYING

adj (kloy ing)

synonyms: profane, blasphemous

It's considered *sacrilegious* for one to enter a mosque wearing shoes.

impious, irreverent toward what is held to be sacred or holy sickly sweet; excessive

When Dave and Liz got together their *cloying* affection towards one another often made their friends ill.

synonyms: excessive, fulsome

SACRILEGIOUS

adj (saak rih lihj uhs)

COAGULATE

verb (koh <u>aag</u> yuh layt)

excessively sweet or sentimental

Geoffrey's *saccharine* poems nauseated Lucy, and she wished he'd stop sending them.

synonyms: maudlin, fulsome

to clot; to cause to thicken

Hemophiliacs can bleed to death from a minor cut because their blood does not *coagulate*.

synonyms: jell, congeal

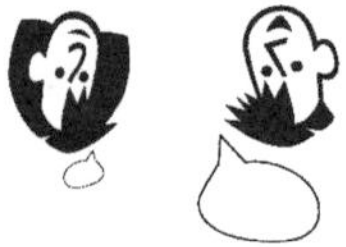

SACCHARINE

adj (saa kuh rihn)

COGENT

adj (<u>koh</u> juhnt)

an elevated platform for public speaking

Though she was terrified, the new member of the debate club approached the *rostrum* with poise.

synonyms: stage, podium

logically forceful; compelling, convincing

> Swayed by the *cogent* argument of the defense, the jury had no choice but to acquit the defendant.

synonyms: persuasive, winning

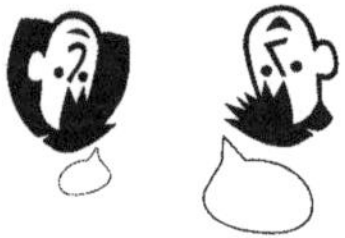

ROSTRUM

noun (rahs truhm)

COLLOQUIAL

adj (kuh loh kwee uhl)

abundant prevalent especially to an increasing degree; filled with

The essay was so *rife* with grammatical errors that it had to be rewritten.

synonyms: numerous, prevailing

characteristic of informal speech

The book was written in a *colloquial* style so it would be more user-friendly.

synonyms: conversational, idiomatic

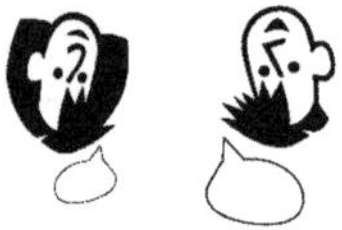

RIFE

adj (rief)

COMMUTE

verb (kuh <u>myoot</u>)

the art of speaking or writing effectively; skill in the effective use of speech

Lincoln's talent for *rhetoric* was evident in his beautifully expressed Gettysburg Address.

synonyms: eloquence, articulateness

to change a penalty to a less severe one

In exchange for cooperating with detectives on another case, the prisoner had his sentence *commuted*.

synonyms: exchange, mitigate

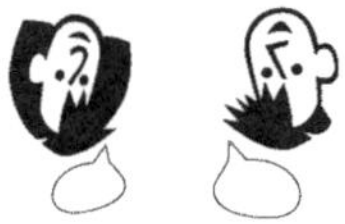

RHETORIC

noun (reh tuhr ihk)

COMPLACENT

adj (kuhm <u>play</u> sihnt)

to criticize with harsh language, verbally abuse

The artist's new installation was *reviled* by critics who weren't used to the departure from his usual work.

synonyms: vituperate, scold, assail

self-satisfied, smug

Alfred always shows a *complacent* smile whenever he wins the spelling bee.

synonyms: contented, unconcerned

REVILE

verb (rih viel)

COMPLIANT

adj (kuhm <u>plie</u> uhnt)

splendid, brilliant

The bride looked *resplendent* in her gown and sparkling tiara.

synonyms: dazzling, bright

submissive, yielding

The boss was unused to an assistant who spoke her mind, but he grew to respect the fact that she wasn't *compliant*.

synonyms: bending, malleable

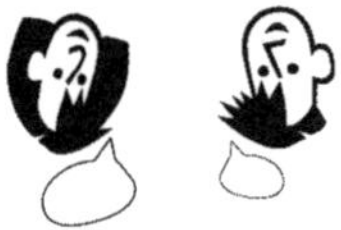

RESPLENDENT

adj (rih splehn duhnt)

CONCOMITANT

adj (kuh <u>kahm</u> ih tuhnt)

marked by firm determination

Louise was *resolute*: She would get into medical school no matter what.

synonyms: firm, unwavering, intent

existing concurrently

A double-major was going to be difficult to pull off, especially since Lucy would have to juggle two papers and two exams *concomitantly*.

synonyms: coexistent, concurrent

RESOLUTE

adj (reh suh loot)

CONCORD

noun (<u>kahn</u> kohrd)

able to recover quickly after illness or bad luck; able to bounce back to shape

Psychologists say that being *resilient* in life is one of the keys to success and happiness.

synonyms: flexible, elastic

agreement

The sisters are now in *concord* about the car they must share.

synonyms: accord, concurrence

RESILIENT

adj (rih sihl yuhnt)

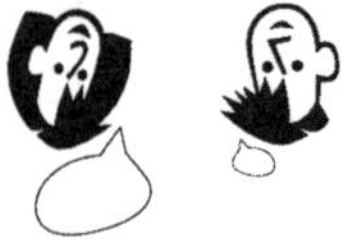

CONDOLE

verb (kuhn dohl)

synonyms: void, annul, revoke

After the celebrity was involved in a scandal, the car company *rescinded* its offer of an endorsement contract.

to repeal, cancel

to grieve; to express sympathy

> My hamster died when I was in third grade, and my friends *condoled* with me and helped bury him in the yard.

synonyms: console, sympathize

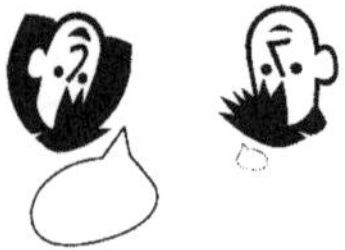

RESCIND

verb (rih sihnd)

CONFLAGRATION

noun (kahn fluh gray shuhn)

to return or repay

Thanks for offering to lend me $1,000, but I know I'll never be able to *requite* your generosity.

synonyms: reciprocate, compensate

big, destructive fire

After the *conflagration* had finally died down, the city center was nothing but a mass of blackened embers.

synonyms: blaze, inferno

REQUITE

verb (rih kwiet)

CONFLUENCE

noun (<u>kahn</u> floo uhns)

to criticize or correct, usually in a gentle manner

Mrs. Hernandez *reproved* her daughter for staying out late and not calling.

synonyms: rebuke, admonish, reprimand

the act of two things flowing together; the junction or meeting place where two things meet

At the political meeting, while planning a demonstration, there was a moving *confluence* of ideas between members.

synonyms: junction, merging

REPROVE

verb (rih proov)

CONSANGUINEOUS

adj (kahn saang gwihn ee uhs)

blameworthy, disreputable

Lowell was thrown out of the bar because of his *reprehensible* behavior toward the other patrons.

synonyms: culpable, deplorable

having the same lineage or ancestry; related by blood

> After having a strange feeling about our relationship for years, I found out that my best friend and I are *consanguineous*.

synonyms: kin, cognate

REPREHENSIBLE

adj (rehp ree hehn suh buhl)

CONSTERNATION

noun (kahn stuhr nay shuhn)

relaxation, leisure

After working hard every day in the busy city, Mike finds his *repose* on weekends playing golf with friends.

synonyms: calmness, tranquility

an intense state of fear or dismay

> One would never think that a seasoned hunter would display such *consternation* when a grizzly bear lumbered too close to camp.

synonyms: cowardice, fear

REPOSE

noun (rih pōhz)

CONSTITUENT

noun (kuhn stih choo uhnt)

abundantly supplied, complete

The gigantic supermarket was *replete* with consumer products of every kind.

synonyms: abounding, full

component, part; citizen, voter

A machine will not function properly if one of its *constituents* is defective.

synonyms: element, factor

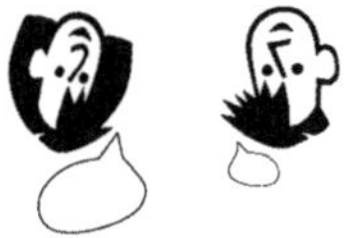

REPLETE

adj (rih pleet)

CONSTRAINT

noun (kuhn <u>straynt</u>)

synonyms: recompense, pay

remuneration.

You can't expect people to do this kind of boring work without some form of

payment for goods or services or to recompense for losses

something that restricts or confines within prescribed bounds

Given the *constraints* of the budget, it was impossible to accomplish my goals.

synonyms: limitation, check

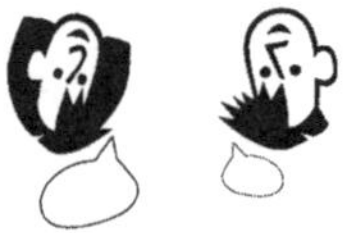

REMUNERATION

noun (rih myoo nuh ray shuhn)

CONTEMPTUOUS

adj (kuhn <u>tehmp</u> choo uhs)

a lessening of intensity or degree

The doctor told me that the disease had gone into *remission*.

synonyms: abatement, subsiding

scornful; expressing contempt

The diners were intimidated by the waiter's *contemptuous* manner.

synonyms: derisive, disdainful, supercilious

REMISSION

noun (rih mih shuhn)

CONTENTIOUS

adj (kuhn <u>tehn</u> shuhs)

to send into exile, banish; assign

Because he hadn't scored any goals during the season, Abe was *relegated* to the bench for the championship game.

synonyms: consign, classify, refer

quarrelsome, disagreeable, belligerent

The *contentious* gentleman in the bar ridiculed anything anyone said.

synonyms: argumentative, fractious, litigious

RELEGATE

verb (rēh luh gāyt)

CONTIGUOUS

adj (kuhn tihg yoo uhs)

to contradict, discredit

She made such a persuasive argument that nobody could *refute* it.

synonym: deny

sharing a boundary; neighboring

> The two houses had *contiguous* yards so the families shared the landscaping expenses.

synonyms: bordering, adjoining

REFUTE

verb (rih fyoot)

CONTINENCE

noun (<u>kahn</u> tih nihns)

to deflect sound or light

The crystal *refracted* the rays of sunlight so they formed a beautiful pattern on the wall.

synonyms: bend, slant

self-control, self-restraint

> Lucy exhibited impressive *continence* in steering clear of fattening foods, and she lost 50 pounds.

synonyms: moderation, discipline

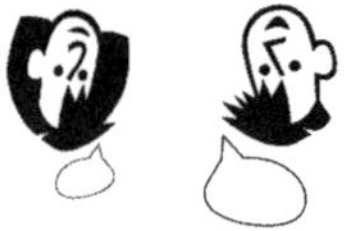

REFRACT

verb (rih fraakt)

CONVALESCE

verb (kahn vuhl ehs)

a tendency to relapse into a previous behavior, especially criminal behavior

According to statistics, the *recidivism* rate for criminals is quite high.

synonyms: return, backslide, relapse

to gradually recover from an illness

After her bout with malaria, Tatiana needed to *convalesce* for a whole month.

synonyms: heal, recuperate

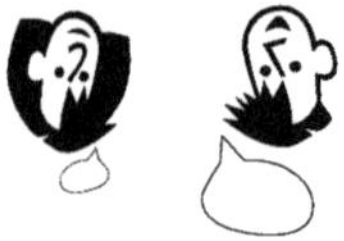

RECIDIVISM
noun (rih sihd uh vih zihm)

CONVERGENCE

noun (kuhn <u>vuhr</u> juhns)

to review by a brief summary

After the long-winded president had finished his speech, his assistant *recapitulated* for the press the points he had made.

synonyms: synopsize, condense, digest

the state of separate elements joining or coming together

A *convergence* of factors led to the tragic unfolding of World War I.

synonyms: union, concurrence, coincidence

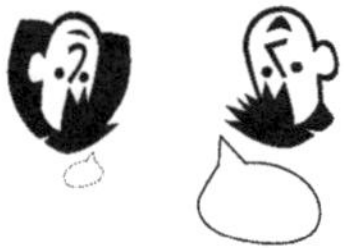

RECAPITULATE

verb (ree kuh pihch yoo layt)

COQUETTE

noun (koh keht)

marked by extreme conservatism, especially in politics

The former radical hippie had turned into quite a *reactionary*, and the press tried to expose her as a hypocrite.

synonyms: ultraconservative, right-wing, orthodox

a flirtatious woman

> The librarian could turn into a *coquette* just by letting her hair down and changing the swing of her hips.

synonym: flirt

REACTIONARY

adj (ree aak shuhn ayr ee)

COTERIE

noun (<u>koh</u> tuh ree)

to tear down, demolish

The house had been *razed*; where it once stood, there was nothing but splinters and bricks.

synonyms: level, destroy

an intimate group of persons with a similar purpose

Judith invited a *coterie* of fellow stamp enthusiasts to a stamp-trading party.

synonyms: clique, set

RAZE

verb (rayz)

COUNTERVAIL

verb (<u>kown</u> tuhr vayl)

synonyms: attenuate, prune

The atmosphere *rarefies* as altitude increases, so the air atop a mountain is too thin to breathe.

to make rare; to make thin or less dense

to act or react with equal force

> In order to *countervail* the financial loss the school suffered after the embezzlement, the treasurer raised the price of room and board.

synonyms: counteract, compensate, offset

RAREFY

verb (rayr uh fie)

COVERT

adj (koh <u>vuhrt</u>)

deeply absorbed

The story was so well performed that the usually rowdy children paid *rapt* attention until the final word.

synonyms: engrossed, immersed

secretive, not openly shown

The *covert* military operation wasn't disclosed until weeks later after it was determined to be a success.

synonym: veiled

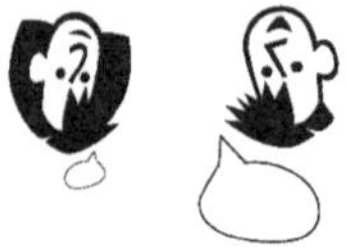

RAPT

adj (raapt)

CULL

verb (kuhl)

taking by force; driven by greed

Sea otters are so *rapacious* that they consume 10 times their body weight in food every day.

synonyms: ravenous, voracious

to select, weed out

You should *cull* the words you need to study from all the flash cards.

synonyms: pick, extract

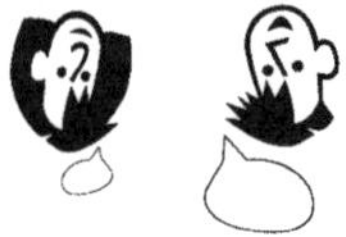

RAPACIOUS

adj (ruh pay shuhs)

to cause anger and irritation

At first the kid's singing was adorable, but after 40 minutes it began to *rankle*.

synonyms: embitter, annoy

CUMULATIVE

adj (<u>kyoom</u> yuh luh tihv)

increasing, collective

> The new employee didn't mind her job at first, but the daily petty indignities had a *cumulative* demoralizing effect.

synonyms: added up, gradual

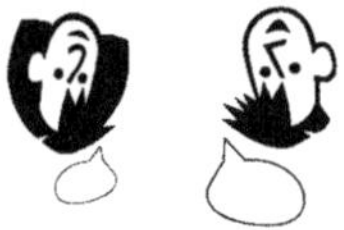

RANKLE

verb (raang kuhl)

bitter hatred

Having been teased mercilessly for years, Herb became filled with *rancor* toward those who had humiliated him.

synonyms: deep-seated ill will

CURT

adj (kuhrt)

abrupt, short with words

The grouchy shop assistant was *curt* with one of her customers, which resulted in a reprimand from her manager.

synonyms: terse, rude

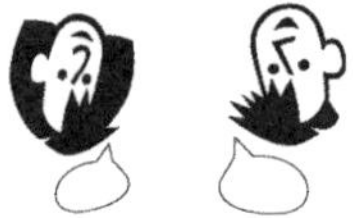

RANCOR

noun (raan kuhr)

DEARTH

noun (duhrth)

to profess, suppose, claim

Brad *purported* to be an opera lover, but he fell asleep at every performance he attended.

synonyms: pretend, purpose

a lack, scarcity, insufficiency

The *dearth* of supplies in our city made it difficult to survive the blizzard.

synonyms: absence, shortage

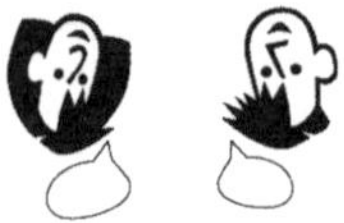

PURPORT

verb (puhr pohrt)

to steal

The amateur detective Dupin found the *purloined* letter for which the police had searched in vain.

synonyms: pilfer, embezzle

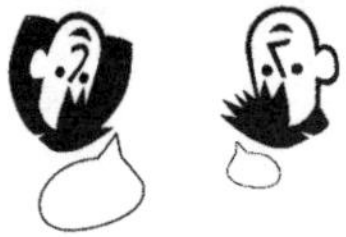

DEBACLE

noun (dih baa kuhl)

a sudden, disastrous collapse or defeat; a total, ridiculous failure

> It was hard for her to show her face in the office after the *debacle* of spilling coffee on her supervisor—three times.

synonyms: crash, wreck

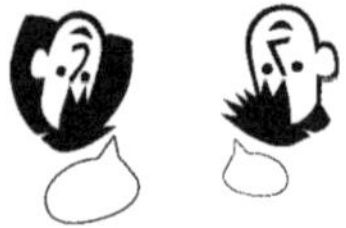

PURLOIN

verb (puhr loyn)

DECLAIM

verb (dih <u>klaym</u>)

one who gives opinions in an authoritative manner

The *pundits* on television are often more entertaining than the sitcoms.

synonym: critic

to speak loudly and vehemently

At Thanksgiving dinner, our grandfather always *declaims* his right, as the eldest, to sit at the head of the table.

synonyms: perorate, rant, rave

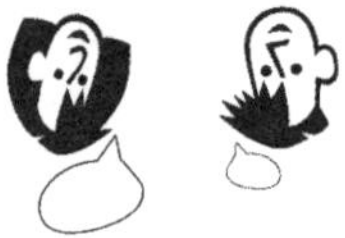

PUNDIT

noun (puhn diht)

DEFAMATORY

adj (dih faam uh tohr ee)

concerned with precise details about codes or conventions

The *punctilious* student never made spelling errors on her essays.

synonyms: precise, scrupulous, meticulous

injurious to the reputation

The tabloid was sued for making *defamatory* statements about the celebrity.

synonyms: libelous, slanderous

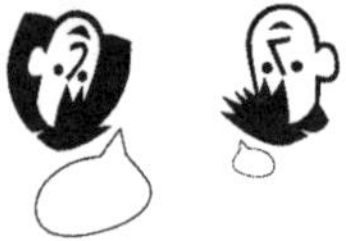

PUNCTILIOUS

adj (puhngk tihl ee uhs)

DEMAGOGUE

noun (<u>deh</u> muh gahg) (<u>deh</u> muh gawg)

powerful

His memoir was full of descriptions of *puissant* military heroics, but most were exaggerations or outright lies.

synonym: strong

leader, rabble-rouser, usually using appeals to emotion or prejudice

Hitler began his political career as a *demagogue*, giving fiery speeches in beer halls.

synonyms: agitator, inciter, instigator

PUISSANT

adj (pwih sihnt) (pyoo sihnt)

DENIZEN

noun (dehn ih zuhn)

boxing

Pugilism has been defended as a positive outlet for aggressive impulses.

synonyms: sparring, fighting

an inhabitant, a resident

The *denizens* of the state understandably wanted to select their own leaders.

synonyms: citizen, habitant, occupant

PUGILISM

noun (pyoo juhl ih suhm)

a fictitious name, used particularly by writers to conceal identity

Though George Eliot sounds as though it's a male name, it was the *pseudonym* that Marian Evans used when she published her classic novel *Middlemarch*.

synonym: pen name

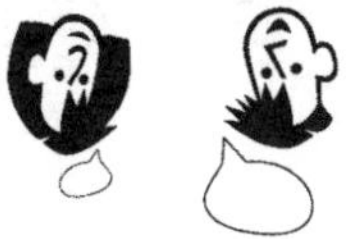

DERIDE

verb (dih <u>ried</u>)

to laugh at contemptuously, to make fun of

As soon as George heard the others *deriding* Anthony, he came to his defense.

synonym: ridicule

PSEUDONYM

noun (soo duh nihm)

DIFFUSE

verb (dih <u>fyooz</u>)

a person authorized to act for someone else

In the event the stock shareholder can't attend the meeting, he'll send a *proxy*.

synonym: representative, alternate

to spread out widely, to scatter freely, to disseminate

> They turned on the fan, but all that did was *diffuse* the cigarette smoke throughout the room.

synonyms: disperse, soften

PROXY

noun (prahk see)

limited in outlook, narrow, unsophisticated

Having grown up in the city, Anita sneered at the *provincial* attitudes of her country cousins.

synonyms: unpolished, unrefined

DIGRESS

verb (die <u>grehs</u>)

to turn aside, especially from the main point; to stray from the subject

The professor repeatedly *digressed* from the topic, boring his students.

synonyms: deviate, wander

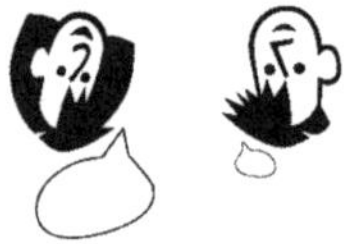

PROVINCIAL

adj (pruh vihn shuhl)

DILAPIDATED

adj (dih <u>laap</u> ih dayt ihd)

lying face downward in adoration or submission

Lying *prostrate* awaiting the Pope, a car splashed me with water.

synonyms: submissive

in disrepair, run down

> Rather than get discouraged, the architect saw great potential in the *dilapidated* house.

synonyms: decayed, fallen into partial ruin

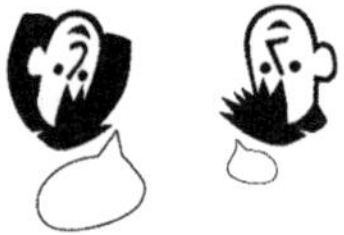

PROSTRATE

adj (prah strayt)

DILUVIAL

adj (dih <u>loo</u> vee uhl)

to condemn or forbid as harmful or unlawful

Consumption of alcohol was *proscribed* in the country's constitution, but the ban was eventually lifted.

synonyms: prohibit, ban

pertaining to a flood

After she left the water running in the house all day, it looked simply *diluvial*.

synonym: waterlogged

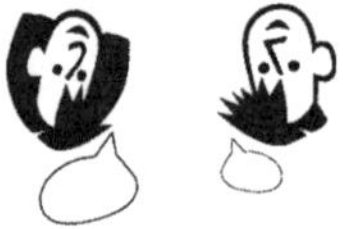

PROSCRIBE

verb (proh skrieb)

DISCOMFIT

verb (dihs <u>kuhm</u> fiht)

relating to prose (as opposed to poetry); dull, ordinary

Simon's *prosaic* style bored his writing teacher to tears, though he thought he had an artistic flair.

synonyms: unimaginative, everyday

to disconcert, to make one lose one's composure

The class clown enjoyed *discomfiting* her classmates whenever possible.

synonyms: embarrass, thwart the plans of

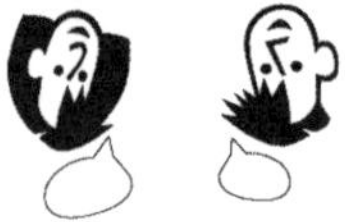

PROSAIC

adj (proh say ihk)

DISCRETE

adj (dih <u>skreet</u>)

A natural inclination or preference

She has a *propensity* for lashing out at others when stressed, so we leave her alone when she's had a rough day.

synonym: tendency

individually distinct, separate

> What's nice about the CD is that each song functions as a *discrete* work and also as part of the whole compilation.

synonyms: unconnected, distinct

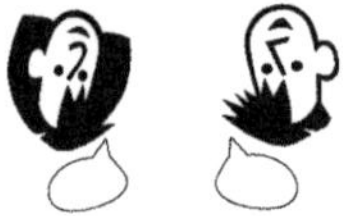

PROPENSITY

noun (proh pehn sih tee)

to make known by open declaration, proclaim

The publicist *promulgated* the idea that the celebrity had indeed gotten married.

synonyms: announce, broadcast

DISINGENUOUS

adj (dihs ihn <u>jehn</u> yoo uhs)

giving a false appearance of simple frankness; misleading

> It was *disingenuous* of him to suggest that he had no idea of the requests made by his campaign contributors.

synonyms: insincere, tricky

PROMULGATE

verb (prah muhl gayt)

DISINTERESTED

adj (dihs <u>ihn</u> trih stihd) (dihs <u>ihn</u> tuh reh stihd)

to grow by rapid production of new parts; increase in number

The cancer cells *proliferated* so quickly that even the doctor was surprised.

synonym: multiply

fair-minded, unbiased

A fair trial is made possible by the selection of *disinterested* jurors.

synonyms: impartial, unprejudiced

PROLIFERATE

verb (proh lih fuhr ayt)

DISPASSIONATE

adj (dihs <u>paash</u> uh niht)

an ancestor in the direct line, forefather; founder

Though his parents had been born here, his *progenitors* were from India.

synonym: inventor

unaffected by bias or strong emotions; not personally or emotionally involved in something

> Ideally, photographers should be *dispassionate* observers of what goes on in the world.

synonyms: disinterested, impartial

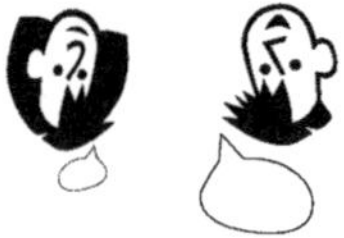

PROGENITOR

noun (proh jehn ih tuhr)

DISSIDENT

adj (<u>dihs</u> ih duhnt)

synonym: propose

The deal *proffered* by the committee satisfied all those at the meeting, ending a month-long discussion.

to offer for acceptance

disagreeing with an established religious or political system

> The *dissident* had been living abroad and writing his criticism of the government from an undisclosed location.

synonym: heretical

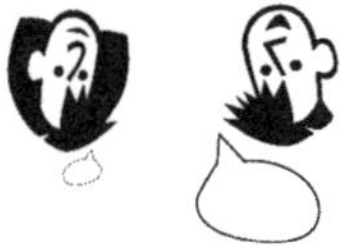

PROFFER

verb (prahf uhr)

recklessly extravagant, wasteful

The *prodigal* expenditures on the military budget during a time of peace created a stir in the Cabinet.

synonym: lavish

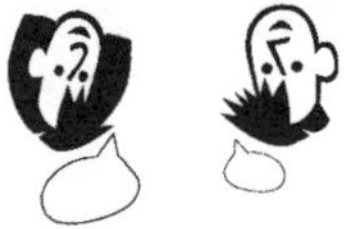

DOCTRINAIRE

adj (dahk truh <u>nayr</u>)

rigidly devoted to theories without regard for practicality; dogmatic

> The professor's manner of teaching was considered *doctrinaire* for such a liberal school.

synonyms: inflexible, dictatorial

PRODIGAL

adj (prah dih guhl)

DOGGED

adj (daw guhd)

ancient, primitive

The archaeologist claimed that the skeleton was of *primeval* origin, though in fact it was the remains of a modern-day monkey.

synonyms: primordial, original

stubbornly persevering

The police inspector's *dogged* determination helped him catch the thief.

synonyms: tenacious, obstinate

PRIMEVAL

adj (priem $\overline{\text{ee}}$ vuhl)

existing outside of nature; extraordinary; supernatural

We were all amazed at her *preternatural* ability to recall smells from her early childhood.

synonyms: psychic, abnormal

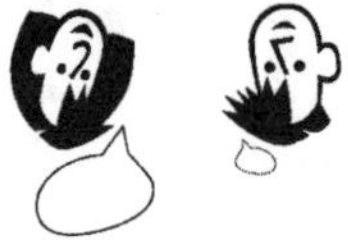

DOLEFUL

adj (<u>dohl</u> fuhl)

sad, mournful

Looking into the *doleful* eyes of the lonely pony, the girl yearned to take him home.

synonyms: dejected, woeful

PRETERNATURAL

adj (pree tuhr naach uhr uhl)

DOUR

adj (doo uhr) (dow uhr)

a cleverly executed trick or deception; sleight of hand

My hunch was that he won the contest not so much as a result of real talent, but rather through *prestidigitation.*

sullen and gloomy; stern and severe

The *dour* hotel concierge demanded payment for the room in advance.

synonyms: austere, strict, grave

PRESTIDIGITATION

noun (prehs tih dihj ih tay shuhn)

EFFLUVIA

noun (ih floo vee uh)

something that foreshadows; a feeling of what will happen in the future

The demolition of the Berlin Wall was a *presage* to the fall of the Soviet Union.

synonym: premonition

waste; odorous fumes given off by waste

> He took out the garbage at 3 AM because the *effluvia* had begun wafting into the bedroom.

synonyms: odor, stench

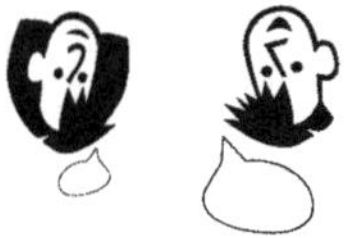

PRESAGE

noun (preh sihj)

ELEGY

noun (<u>eh</u> luh jee)

steeply; hastily

At the sight of the approaching helicopters, Private Johnson *precipitously* shot a flare into the air.

synonyms: impetuous, headlong, reckless

a mournful poem, usually about the dead

A memorable *elegy* was read aloud for the spiritual leader.

synonyms: memorial, lament

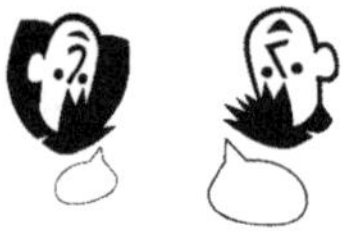

PRECIPITOUSLY

adv (prih sihp ih tuhs lee)

ELUDE

verb (ih lood)

synonyms: doubtful, chancy

Given the *precarious* circumstances, I chose to opt out of the deal completely.

lacking in security or stability; dependent on chance or uncertain conditions to avoid cleverly, to escape the perception of

Somehow, the runaway *eluded* detection for weeks.

synonyms: evade, dodge

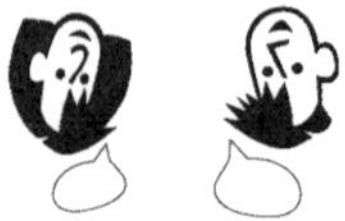

PRECARIOUS

adj (prih caa ree uhs)

EMOLLIENT

adj (ih mohl yuhnt)

a ruler; one who wields great power

Alex was much kinder before he assumed the role of *potentate*.

synonyms: leader, dominator

soothing, especially to the skin

> After being out in the sun for so long, the *emollient* cream was a welcome relief on my skin.

synonyms: softening, mollifying

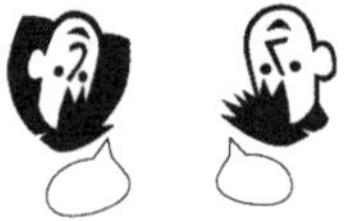

POTENTATE

noun (poh tehn tayt)

EMULATE

verb (<u>ehm</u> yuh layt)

suitable for drinking

Though the water was *potable*, it tasted terrible.

synonym: unpolluted

to strive to equal or excel, to imitate

Children often *emulate* their parents.

synonyms: follow, mimic

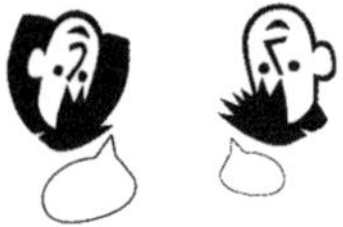

POTABLE

adj (pōh tuh buhl)

ENCUMBER

verb (ehn <u>kuhm</u> buhr)

to assume as real or conceded; propose as an explanation

Before proving the math formula, we need to *posit* that *x* and *y* are real numbers.

synonym: suggest

to weigh down, to burden

> She often felt *encumbered* by the distractions of the city, so she sought a quieter place in the country.

synonyms: hamper, oppress, saddle

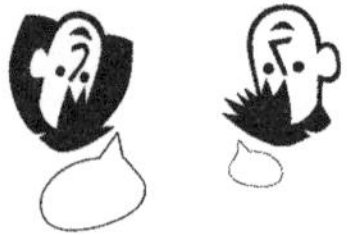

POSIT

verb (pohz iht)

ENJOIN

verb (ehn joyn)

foreshadowing, ominous; eliciting amazement and wonder

Everyone thought the rays of light were *portentous* until they realized a nine-year-old was playing a joke on them.

synonym: premonitory

to direct or impose with urgent appeal, to order with emphasis; to forbid

> Patel is *enjoined* by his culture from eating the flesh of a cow, which is sacred in India.

synonyms: instruct, charge

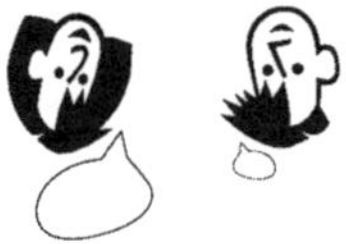

PORTENTOUS

adj (pohr tehn tuhs)

EPOCHAL

adj (<u>ehp</u> uh kuhl) (ehp <u>ahk</u> uhl)

to read studiously or attentively

I've *pored* over this text, yet I still can't understand it.

synonyms: stare, ponder

momentous, highly significant

> The Supreme Court's *epochal* decision will no doubt affect generations to come.

synonyms: unparalleled, notable

PORE

verb (pohr)

EPONYMOUS

adj (ih pahn uh muhs)

a speaker of many languages

Ling's extensive travels have helped her to become a true *polyglot*.

giving one's name to a place, book, restaurant

Macbeth was the *eponymous* protagonist of Shakespeare's play.

synonym: named after

POLYGLOT

noun (pah lee glaht)

EQUIVOCATE

verb (ih <u>kwihv</u> uh kayt)

shrewd and crafty in managing or dealing with things

She was wise to curb her tongue and was able to explain her problem to the judge in a respectful and *politic* manner.

synonym: tactful

to avoid committing oneself in what one says, to be deliberately unclear

> Not wanting to implicate himself in the crime, the suspect *equivocated* for hours.

synonyms: lie, mislead

POLITIC

adj (pah lih tihk)

ERSATZ

adj (uhr sahtz)

courageous; spunky

The *plucky* young nurse dove into the foxhole, determined to help the wounded soldier.

synonym: brave

being an artificial and inferior substitute or imitation

The *ersatz* strawberry shortcake tasted more like plastic than like real cake.

synonyms: fake, counterfeit

PLUCKY

adj (pluh kee)

crude or coarse; characteristic of commoners

After five weeks of rigorous studying, the graduate settled in for a weekend of *plebeian* socializing and television watching.

synonyms: unrefined, conventional

ESCHEW

verb (ehs <u>choo</u>)

to shun; to avoid (as something wrong or distasteful)

> The filmmaker *eschewed* artifical light for her actors, resulting in a stark movie style.

synonyms: evade, escape

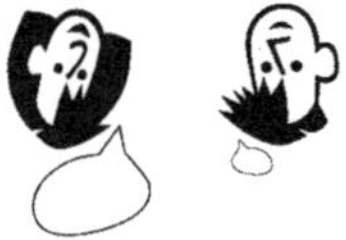

PLEBEIAN

adj (plee bee uhn)

ESPOUSE

verb (ih spowz)

synonym: cliché

Instead of the usual *platitudes*, the comedian gave a memorable and inspiring speech to the graduating class.

overused and trite remark

to take up and support as a cause; to marry

> Because of his religious beliefs, the preacher could not *espouse* the use of capital punishment.

synonyms: champion, adopt

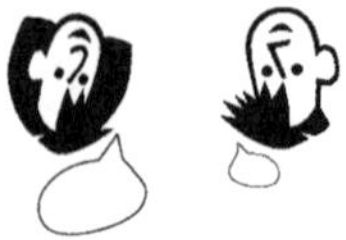

PLATITUDE

noun (plaa tih tood)

ESPY

verb (ehs pie)

synonyms: mournful, sorrowful

The *plaintive* cries from the girl trapped in the tree were heard by all.

expressive of suffering or woe, melancholy

to catch sight of, glimpse

Amidst a crowd in black clothing, she *espied* the colorful dress that her friend was wearing.

synonym: discern

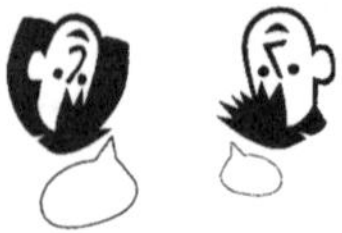

PLAINTIVE

adj (playn tihv)

EUPHEMISM

noun (yoo fuh mihz uhm)

to arouse anger or resentment in; provoke

His continual insensitivity *piqued* my anger.

synonyms: irritate, rouse

an inoffensive and agreeable expression that is substituted for one that is considered offensive

The funeral director preferred to use the *euphemism* “passed away” instead of the word “died.”

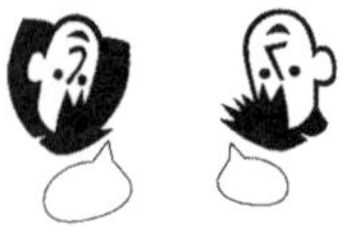

PIQUE

verb (peek)

EUTHANASIA

noun (yoo thun <u>nay</u> zhuh)

having a sluggish, unemotional temperament

His writing was energetic but his *phlegmatic* personality wasn't suited for television, so he turned down the interview.

synonyms: matter-of-fact, undemonstrative

the practice of ending the life of hopelessly ill individuals; assisted suicide

Euthanasia has always been the topic of much moral debate.

synonym: mercy-killing

PHLEGMATIC

adj (flehg maa tihk)

EXCORIATE

verb (ehk skohr ee ayt)

the study of ancient texts and languages

Philology was the predecessor to modern-day linguistics.

to censure scathingly; to express strong disapproval of

> The three-page letter to the editor *excoriated* the publication for printing the rumor without verifying the source.

synonym: denounce

PHILOLOGY

noun (fih lahl uh jee)

EXPONENT

noun (ehk spoh nuhnt)

a person who is guided by materialism and is disdainful of intellectual or artistic values

The *philistine* never even glanced at the rare violin in his collection but instead kept an eye on its value and sold it at a profit.

one who champions or advocates

The vice president was an enthusiastic *exponent* of computer technology.

synonyms: supporter, representative

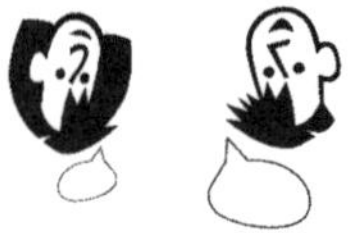

PHILISTINE

noun (fihl uh steen)

EXPOUND

verb (ihk <u>spownd</u>)

a compact or close-knit body of people, animals, or things

A *phalanx* of guards stood outside the prime minister's home day and night.

synonyms: mass, legion

to explain or describe in detail

The teacher *expounded* on the theory of relativity for hours.

synonyms: elucidate, elaborate

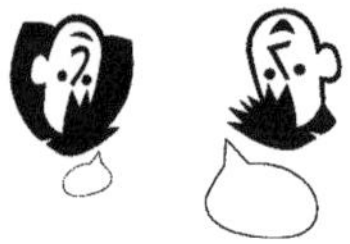

PHALANX

noun (fay laanks)

EXPUNGE

verb (ihk <u>spuhnj</u>)

synonyms: walk, traverse

It has always been a dream of mine to *peregrinate* from one side of Europe to the other with nothing but a backpack.

to travel on foot

to erase, eliminate completely

> The parents' association *expunged* the questionable texts from the children's reading list.

synonyms: delete, obliterate

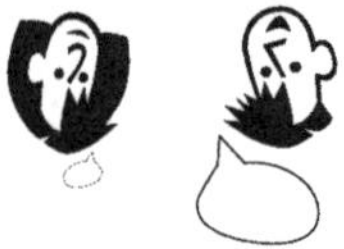

PEREGRINATE

verb (pehr ih gruh nayt)

EXTIRPATE

verb (ehk stuhr payt)

an oppressive lack of resources (as money), severe poverty

Once a famous actor, he eventually died in *penury* and anonymity.

synonyms: destitution, impoverishment

to root out, eradicate, literally or figuratively; to destroy wholly

The terrorist cells were *extirpated* after many years of investigation.

synonym: wipe out

PENURY

noun (pehn yuh ree)

EXTRAPOLATION

noun (ihk strap uh lay shuhn)

expressing sorrow for sins or offenses, repentant

Claiming the murderer did not feel *penitent*, the victim's family felt his pardon should be denied.

synonyms: remorseful, apologetic

the process of using known data and information to determine what will happen in the future

> Through the process of *extrapolation*, we were able to determine which mutual funds to invest in.

synonyms: projection, forecast

PENITENT

adj (pehn ih tuhnt)

EXTRINSIC

adj (ihk strihn sihk) (ihk strihn zihk)

synonyms: leaning, predilection

After Daniel visited the Grand Canyon, he developed a *penchant* for travel.

an inclination, a definite liking

external, unessential; originating from the outside

> "Though they are interesting to note," the meeting manager claimed, "those facts are *extrinsic* to the matter under discussion."

synonyms: extraneous, foreign

PENCHANT

noun (pehn chuhnt)

EXTRUDE

verb (ihk <u>strood</u>)

transparently clear in style or meaning, easy to understand

Though she thought she could hide her ulterior motives, they were *pellucid* to everyone else.

synonym: apparent

to form or shape something by pushing it out, to force out, especially through a small opening

We watched in awe as the volcano *extruded* molten lava.

synonym: squeeze out

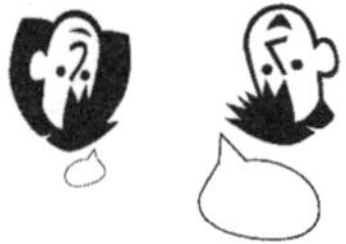

PELLUCID

adj (peh loo sihd)

relating to money

Michelle's official title was office manager, but she ended up taking on a lot of *pecuniary* responsibilities such as payroll duties.

synonym: fiscal, financial

FACETIOUS

adj (fuh <u>see</u> shuhs)

witty, humorous

Her *facetious* remarks made the uninteresting meeting more lively.

synonyms: amusing, comical

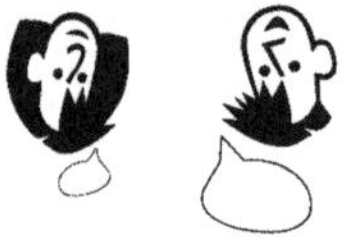

PECUNIARY

adj (pih kyoon nee ehr ee)

FACILE

adj (faa suhl)

to embezzle

These days in the news, we read more and more about workers *peculating* the system.

synonym: misappropriate

easily accomplished; seeming to lack sincerity or depth; arrived at without due effort

Given the complexity of the problem, it seemed a rather *facile* solution.

synonyms: effortless, superficial

PECULATE

verb (pehk yuh layt)

FALLACIOUS

adj (fuh <u>lay</u> shuhs)

to act as patron of, to adopt an air of condescension toward; to buy from

LuAnn *patronized* the students, treating them like simpletons, which they deeply resented.

synonym: condescend

tending to deceive or mislead; based on a fallacy

The *fallacious* statement "the Earth is flat" misled people for many years.

synonyms: false, erroneous

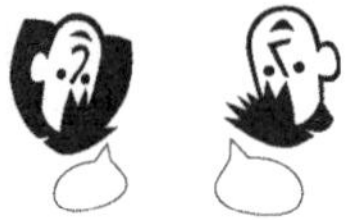

PATRONIZE

verb (pay truh niez)

aristocratic

Though he really couldn't afford an expensive lifestyle, Claudius had *patrician* tastes.

synonym: high-class

FEBRILE

adj (<u>fehb</u> ruhl) (<u>fee</u> bruhl)

feverish, marked by intense emotion or activity

> Awaiting the mysterious announcement, there was a *febrile* excitement in the crowd.

synonyms: agitated, flushed

PATRICIAN

adj (puh trih shuhn)

causing disease

Bina's research on the origins of *pathogenic* microorganisms should help stop the spread of disease.

synonyms: noxious, infecting

FECKLESS

adj (<u>fehk</u> lihs)

ineffective, worthless

Anja took on the responsibility of caring for her aged mother, realizing that her *feckless* sister was not up to the task.

synonym: incompetent

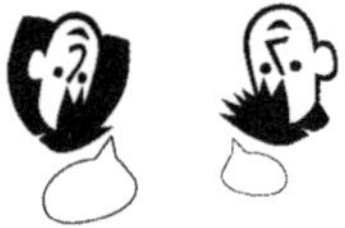

PATHOGENIC

adj (paa thuh jehn ihk)

FEIGN

verb (fayn)

obvious, evident

Moe could no longer stand Frank's *patent* fawning over the boss and so confronted him.

synonyms: unconcealed, clear

to pretend, to give a false appearance of

Though she had discovered they were planning a party, she *feigned* surprise so as not to spoil the festivities.

synonym: fake

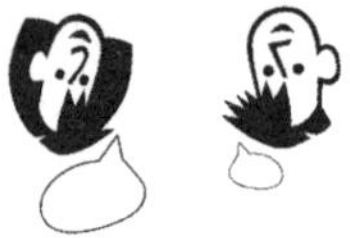

PATENT

adj (paa tehnt)

an outcast

Once he betrayed those in his community, he was banished and lived the life of a *pariah*.

synonyms: untouchable, abomination

FERAL

adj (<u>fehr</u> uhl)

suggestive of a wild beast, not domesticated

> Though the animal-rights activists did not want to see the *feral* dogs harmed, they offered no solution to the problem.

synonym: wild, savage

PARIAH

noun (puh rīe ah)

to trim off excess, reduce

The cook's hands were sore after she *pared* hundreds of potatoes for the banquet.

synonyms: peel, clip

FICTIVE

adj (<u>fihk</u> tihv)

fictional, relating to imaginative creation

> She found she was more productive when writing *fictive* stories rather than autobiography.

synonym: not genuine

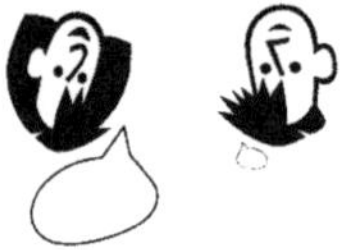

PARE

verb (payr)

supreme, of chief importance

It's of *paramount* importance that we make it back to camp before the storm hits.

synonyms: primary, dominant

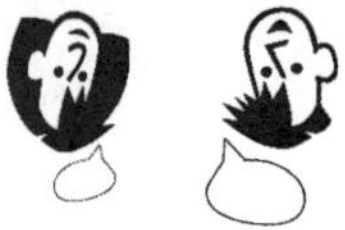

FILIBUSTER

verb (fihl ih buhs tuhr)

to use obstructionist tactics, especially prolonged speech making, in order to delay something

> The congressman read names from the phonebook in an attempt to *filibuster* a pending bill.

synonym: stall

PARAMOUNT

adj (paar uh mownt)

FITFUL

adj (<u>fiht</u> fuhl)

a model of excellence or perfection

She's the *paragon* of what a judge should be: honest, intelligent, and just.

synonyms: ideal, paradigm

intermittent, lacking steadiness; characterized by irregular bursts of activity

> Her *fitful* breathing became cause for concern, and eventually, she phoned the doctor.

synonyms: sporadic, periodic

PARAGON

noun (paar uh gahn)

FLIPPANT

adj (<u>flihp</u> uhnt)

an outstandingly clear or typical example

The new restaurant owner used the fast-food giant as a *paradigm* for expansion into new locales.

synonym: model

marked by disrespectful lightheartedness or casualness

> Her *flippant* response was unacceptable and she was asked again to explain herself.

synonyms: pert, disrespectful

PARADIGM

noun (paar uh diem)

FLOUT

verb (flowt)

synonyms: compliment, homage

The director's *panegyric* for the donor who kept his charity going was heart-warming.

elaborate praise; formal hymn of praise

to scorn, to disregard with contempt

The protestors *flouted* the committee's decision and hoped to sway public opinion.

synonyms: mock, sneer, spurn

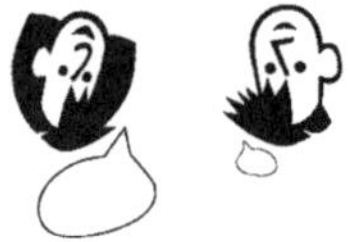

PANEGYRIC
noun (paan uh geer ihk)

FODDER

noun (fahd uhr)

synonyms: general, extensive

Pandemic alarm spread throughout Colombia after the devastating earthquake.

occurring over a wide geographic area and affecting a large portion of the population raw material, as for artistic creation; readily abundant ideas or images

The governor's hilarious blunder was good *fodder* for the comedian.

synonym: material

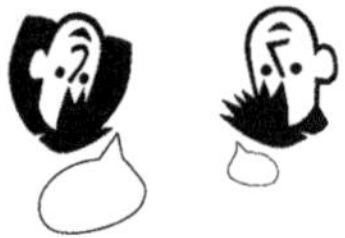

PANDEMIC

adj (paan deh mihk)

flamboyance or dash in style and action

Leah has such *panache* when planning parties, even when they're last-minute affairs.

synonym: flair

FOREGO

verb (fohr <u>goh</u>)

to precede, to go ahead of

> Because of the risks of the expedition, the team leader made sure to *forego* the climbers.

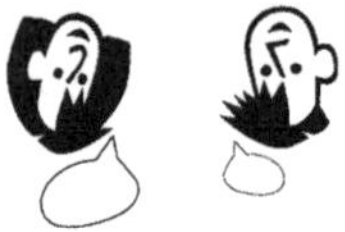

PANACHE

noun (puh nahsh)

FORGO

verb (fohr goh)

synonyms: trifling, petty

all the way to the hotel.

Bernardo paid the ragged boy the *paltry* sum of 25 cents to carry his luggage

pitifully small or worthless

to do without, to abstain from

As much as I wanted to *forgo* statistics, I knew it would serve me well in my field of study.

synonym: pass on

PALTRY

adj (pawl tree)

FORMIDABLE

adj (fohr mih duh buhl) (fohr mih duh buhl)

capable of being touched or felt; easily perceived

The tension was *palpable* as I walked into the room.

synonyms: readily detected, tangible

fearsome, daunting; tending to inspire awe or wonder

> The wrestler was not very big, but his skill and speed made him a *formidable* opponent.

synonym: overpowering

PALPABLE

adj (paalp uh buhl)

FORTITUDE

noun (fohr tih tood)

an object or place having diverse layers or aspects beneath the surface

Years ago, paper was very expensive, so the practice was to write over previous words, creating a *palimpsest* of writing.

strength of mind that allows one to encounter adversity with courage

Months in the trenches exacted great *fortitude* of the soldiers.

synonyms: endurance, courage

PALIMPSEST

noun (paal ihmp sehst)

FORTUITOUS

adj (fohr too ih tuhs)

relating to a palace; magnificent

After living in a cramped studio apartment for years, Alicia thought the modest one bedroom looked downright *palatial*.

synonyms: grand, stately

by chance, especially by favorable chance

After a *fortuitous* run-in with an agent, Roxy won a recording contract.

synonym: accidental

PALATIAL

adj (puh lay shuhl)

FRENETIC

adj (fruh <u>neht</u> ihk)

a tribute, a song or expression of praise

He considered his newest painting a *paean* to his late wife.

frantic, frenzied

The employee's *frenetic* schedule left him little time to socialize.

synonym: feverish

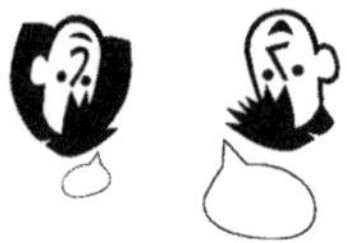

PAEAN

noun (pee uhn)

to remove from position by force; eject

After President Nixon so offensively lied to the country during Watergate, he was *ousted* from office.

synonyms: dismiss, evict

FULSOME

adj (fool suhm)

abundant; flattering in an insincere way

The king's servant showered him with *fulsome* compliments in hopes of currying favor.

synonyms: insincere, saccharine

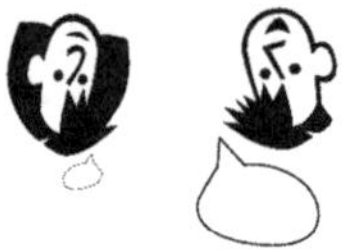

OUST
verb (owst)

to exclude from a group by common consent

Feeling *ostracized* from her friends, Tabitha couldn't figure out what she had done.

synonyms: isolate, excommunicate

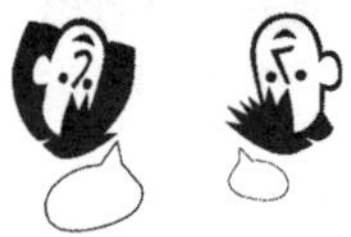

FURLOUGH

noun (fuhr loh)

a leave of absence, especially granted to soldier or a prisoner

After seeing months of combat, the soldier received a much-deserved *furlough*.

synonym: time off

OSTRACIZE

verb (ahs truh siez)

FURTIVE

adj (fuhr tihv)

to change into bone; to become hardened or set in a rigidly conventional pattern

The forensics expert ascertained the body's age based on the degree to which the facial structure had *ossified*.

sly, with hidden motives

> The *furtive* glances they exchanged made me suspect they were up to something.

synonyms: secret, surreptitious

OSSIFY

verb (ah sih fie)

GALVANIZE

verb (<u>gaal</u> vuh niez)

to swing back and forth like a pendulum; to vary between opposing beliefs or feelings

The move meant a new house in a lovely neighborhood, but she missed her friends, so she *oscillated* between joy and sadness.

synonyms: fluctuate, vary

to shock; to arouse awareness

The closing down of another homeless shelter *galvanized* the activist group into taking political action.

synonyms: vitalize, energize

OSCILLATE

verb (ah sihl ayt)

GAMELY

adj (gaym lee)

synonyms: disagreeable, unfriendly

My first impression of the taxi driver was that he was *ornery*, but then he explained that he'd just had a bad day.

having an irritable disposition, cantankerous

spiritedly, bravely

> The park ranger *gamely* navigated the trail up the steepest face of the mountain.

synonym: excitedly

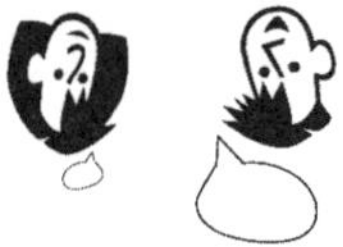

ORNERY

adj (ohr nuh ree)

GAUCHE

adj (gohsh)

disgraceful, shameful

She wrote an *opprobrious* editorial in the newspaper about the critic who tore her new play to shreds.

synonym: scornful

lacking social refinement

Snapping one's fingers to get the waiter's attention is considered *gauche*.

synonyms: tactless, simple

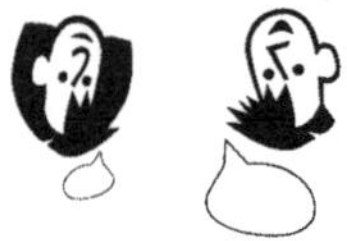

OPPROBRIOUS

adj (uh proh bree uhs)

GRANDILOQUENCE

noun (graan dihl uh kwuhns)

one who takes advantage of any opportunity to achieve an end, with little regard for principles

The *opportunist* wasted no time in stealing the idea and presenting it as his own.

synonyms: user, self-seeker

pompous talk; fancy but meaningless language

> The headmistress was notorious for her *grandiloquence* at the lectern and her ostentatious clothes.

synonyms: bravado, pretension

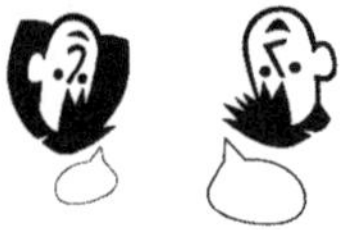

OPPORTUNIST

noun (ahp uhr too nihst)

GREGARIOUS

adj (greh gayr ee uhs)

to express an opinion

At the "Let's Chat Talk Show," the audience member *opined* that the guest was in the wrong.

synonyms: point out, voice

outgoing, sociable

Unlike her introverted friends, Susan was very *gregarious*.

synonyms: convivial, friendly

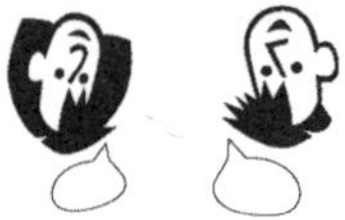

OPINE

verb (oh pīen)

GROTTO

noun (grah toh)

a burden, an obligation

Antonia was beginning to feel the *onus* of having to feed her friend's cat for the month.

synonyms: responsibility, hardship

a small cave

Alone on the island, Philoctetes sought shelter in a *grotto*.

synonyms: cavern, recess, burrow

ONUS

noun (ōh nuhs)

HARANGUE

verb (huh raang)

a government in which a small group exercises supreme control

In an *oligarchy*, the few who rule are generally wealthier and have more status than the others.

synonym: small government

to give a long speech

Maria's parents *harangued* her when she told them she'd spent her money on magic beans.

synonyms: lecture, reprimand

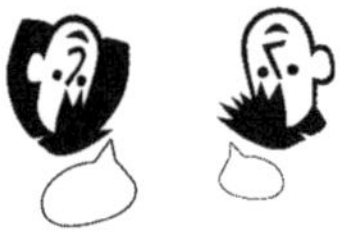

OLIGARCHY

noun (ōh lih gaar kee)

HEDONIST

noun (<u>hee</u> duhn ihst)

synonyms: fragrant, odorous

Whenever she entered a candle store, her *olfactory* sense was awakened.

relating to the sense of smell

one who pursues pleasure as a goal

Michelle, an admitted *hedonist*, lays on the couch eating cookies every Saturday.

synonyms: pleasure-seeker, glutton

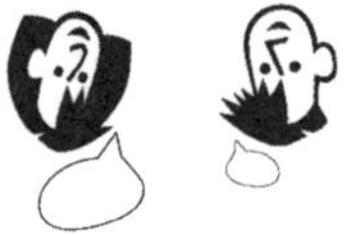

OLFACTORY

adj (ohl faak tuh ree)

HEGEMONY

noun (hih <u>jeh</u> muh nee)

unreasonably persistent

The *obstinate* journalist would not reveal his source, and thus, was jailed for 30 days.

synonyms: stubborn, headstrong

the domination of one state or group over its allies

When Germany claimed *hegemony* over Russia, Stalin was outraged.

synonyms: power, authority

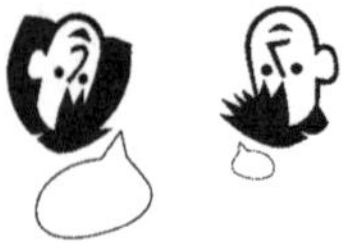

OBSTINATE

adj (ahb stih nuht)

HERETICAL

adj (huh <u>reh</u> tih kuhl)

synonyms: shadow, complicate

Benny always *obfuscates* the discussion by bringing in irrelevant facts.

to confuse, make obscure

departing from accepted beliefs or standards, oppositional

> At the onset of the Inquisition, the *heretical* priest was forced to flee the country.

synonym: unorthodox

OBFUSCATE

verb (ahb fyoo skayt)

HIATUS

noun (hie ay tuhs)

stubbornly persistent, resistant to persuasion

The president was *obdurate* on the matter, and no amount of public protest could change his mind.

synonyms: inflexible, inexorable, adamant

a gap or interruption in space, time, or continuity

> After a long *hiatus* in Greece, the philosophy professor returned to the university.

synonym: break

OBDURATE

adj (ahb duhr uht)

HISTRIONICS

noun (hihs tree ahn ihks)

new and not resembling anything formerly known

Piercing any part of the body other than the earlobes was *novel* in the 1950s, but now it is quite common.

synonyms: original, innovative

deliberate display of emotion for effect; exaggerated behavior calculated for effect

With such *histrionics*, she should really consider becoming an actress.

synonyms: melodrama, theatrics

NOVEL

adj (nah vuhl)

a statement that does not follow logically from anything previously said

After the heated political debate, her comment about cake was a real *non sequitur*.

synonyms: illogical argument, off-topic comment

HUBRIS

noun (hyoo brihs)

excessive pride or self-confidence

Nathan's *hubris* spurred him to do things that many considered insensitive.

sysnonyms: presumption, arrogance

NON SEQUITUR

noun (nahn sehk wih tuhr)

HUSBAND

verb (huhz buhnd)

a system of scientific names

In botany class, we learned the *nomenclature* used to identify different species of roses.

synonyms: classification, codification

to manage economically; to use sparingly

> The cyclist paced herself at the start of the race, knowing that if she *husbanded* her resources she'd have the strength to break out of the pack later on.

synonym: conserve

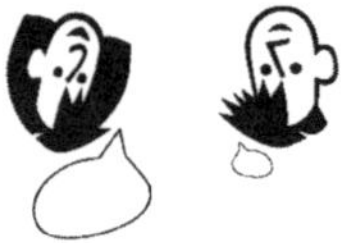

NOMENCLATURE

noun (noh muhn klay chuhr)

belief that traditional values and beliefs are unfounded and that existence is useless; belief that conditions in the social organization are so bad as to make destruction desirable

> Robert's *nihilism* expressed itself in his lack of concern with the norms of moral society.

synonyms: skepticism, terrorism

HYPOCRITE

noun (<u>hih</u> puh kriht)

one who puts on a false appearance of virtue; one who criticizes a flaw he in fact possesses

> What a *hypocrite*: He criticizes those who wear fur but then he buys for himself a leather shearling coat.

synonyms: pretender, deceiver

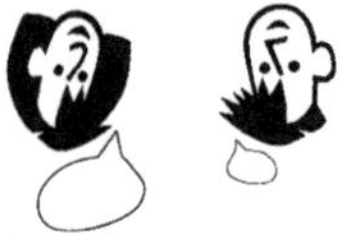

NIHILISM

noun (nie hihl ihz uhm)

IGNOBLE

adj (ihg noh buhl)

a newborn child

The *neonate* was born prematurely so she's still in the hospital.

synonyms: baby, infant

having low moral standards, not noble in character; mean

The photographer was paid a princely sum for the picture of the self-proclaimed ethicist in the *ignoble* act of pick-pocketing.

synonyms: lowly, vulgar

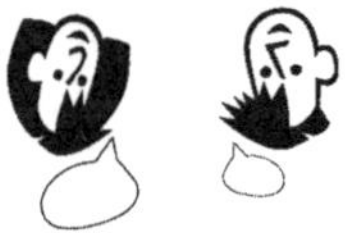

NEONATE

noun (nee uh nayt)

ILLUSORY

adj (ih loo suhr ee) (ih loos ree)

intensely wicked or vicious

Nefarious deeds are never far from an evil-doer's mind.

synonyms: malevolent, sinister

producing illusion, deceptive

> The desert explorer was devastated to discover that the lake he thought he had seen was in fact *illusory*.

synonyms: false, imaginary

NEFARIOUS

adj (nih fahr ee uhs)

the practice of communicating with the dead in order to predict the future

The practice of *necromancy* supposes belief in survival of the soul after death.

synonyms: sorcery, black magic

IMBIBE

verb (ihm bieb)

to receive into the mind and take in

If I always attend class, I can *imbibe* as much knowledge as possible.

synonym: absorb

NECROMANCY

noun (nehk ruh maan see)

IMPASSIVE

adj (ihm <u>paas</u> sihv)

vague, undefined

The candidate's *nebulous* plans to fight crime made many voters skeptical.

synonyms: hazy, unclear

absent of any external sign of emotion, expressionless

> Given his *impassive* expression, it was hard to tell whether he approved of my plan.

synonyms: apathetic, unemotional

NEBULOUS

adj (neh byoo luhs)

IMPERIOUS

adj (ihm <u>pihr</u> ee uhs)

lacking foresight, having a narrow view or long-range perspective

Not wanting to spend a lot of money up front, the *myopic* business owner would likely suffer the consequences later.

synonyms: short-sighted, unthinking

commanding, domineering; urgent

> Though the king had been a kind leader, his daughter was *imperious* and demanding during her rule.

synonym: authoritarian

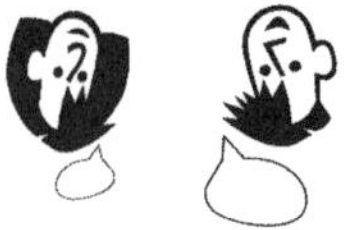

MYOPIC

adj (mie ahp ihk) (mie oh pihk)

IMPERTURBABLE

adj (<u>ihm</u> puhr <u>tuhr</u> buh buhl)

the quality of being capable of change, in form or character; susceptibility of change

The actress lacked the *mutability* needed to perform in the improvisational play.

synonyms: inconstancy, variation

unshakably calm and steady

No matter how disruptive the children became, the babysitter remained *imperturbable.*

synonyms: cool, unflappable

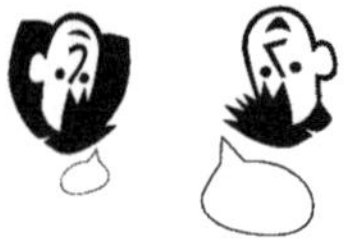

MUTABILITY

noun (myoo tuh bihl uh tee)

IMPLACABLE

adj (ihm play kuh buhl) (ihm plaa kuh buhl)

synonyms: bit, shred

Monica's eye watered, irritated by a *mote* of dust.

a small particle, speck

inflexible; not capable of being changed or pacified

The *implacable* teasing was hard for the child to take.

synonyms: merciless, relentless

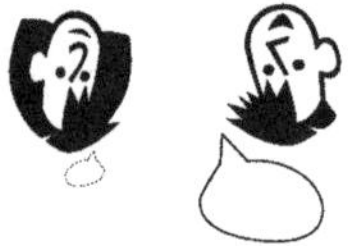

MOTE

noun (moht)

IMPORTUNATE

adj (ihm pohr chuh niht)

gloomy, sullen

After hearing that the internship had been given to someone else, Lenny was *morose* for days.

synonyms: pessimistic, dour

troublesomely urgent; extremely persistent in request or demand

Her *importunate* appeal for a job caused me to grant her an interview.

synonyms: insistent, obstinate

MOROSE

adj (muh rohs) (maw rohs)

IMPRECATION

noun (ihm prih kay shuhn)

fixed customs or manners; moral attitudes

In keeping with the *mores* of ancient Roman society, Nero held a celebration every weekend.

synonyms: conventions, practices

a curse

> Spouting violent *imprecations*, Hank searched for the person who had vandalized his truck.

synonym: damnation

MORES

noun (mawr ayz)

IMPUDENT

adj (<u>ihm</u> pyuh duhnt)

biting and caustic in manner and style

Roald Dahl's stories are *mordant* alternatives to bland kids' stories.

synonyms: scathing, hurtful

marked by cocky boldness or disregard for others

> Considering the judge had been lenient in her sentence, it was *impudent* of the defendant to refer to her by her first name.

synonyms: arrogant, insolent

MORDANT

adj (mohr dnt)

IMPUGN

verb (ihm pyoon)

synonyms: pacify, appease

to soothe in temper or disposition

A small raise and increased break time *mollified* the unhappy staff, at least for the moment.

to call into question; to attack verbally

> "How dare you *impugn* my motives?" protested the lawyer, on being accused of ambulance chasing.

synonyms: challenge, dispute

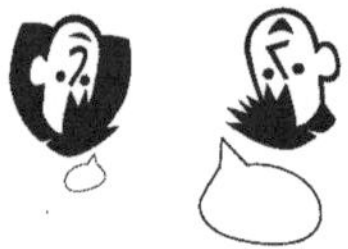

MOLLIFY

verb (mahl uh fie)

IMPUTE

verb (ihm <u>pyoot</u>)

a small portion, limited quantity

I expect at least a *modicum* of assistance from you on the day of the party.

synonyms: crumb, iota

to lay the responsibility or blame for, often unjustly

> It seemed unfair to *impute* the accident on me, especially since they were the ones who ran the red light.

synonyms: ascribe, attribute, pin on

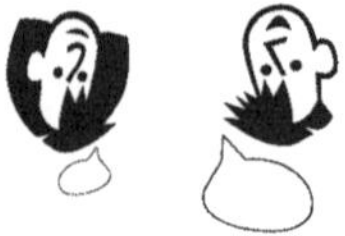

MODICUM

noun (mahd ih kuhm)

INCANDESCENT

adj (ihn kuhn dehs uhnt)

to make less severe, make milder

A judge may *mitigate* a sentence if it's decided that the crime was committed out of necessity.

synonyms: relieve, alleviate

shining brightly

The *incandescent* glow of the moon made it a night I'll never forget.

synonyms: brilliant, radiant

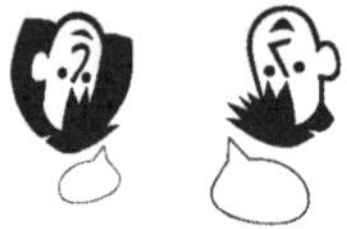

MITIGATE

verb (miht ih gayt)

INCARNADINE

adj (ihn kaar nuh dien) (ihn kaar nuh dihn)

a written note or letter

Priscilla spent hours composing a romantic *missive* for Elvis.

synonym: message

red, especially blood red

The *incarnadine* lipstick she wore made her look much older than she was.

synonym: sanguine

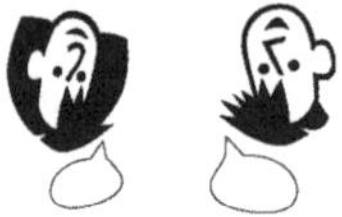

MISSIVE

noun (mihs ihv)

INCHOATE

adj (ihn <u>koh</u> iht)

synonyms: error, misapplication

Iceland is a *misnomer* since it isn't really icy; the name means "island."

an error in naming a person or place

being only partly in existence; imperfectly formed

For every page of the crisp writing that made it into the final book, Jessie has 10 pages of *inchoate* rambling that made up the first draft.

synonyms: formless, undefined

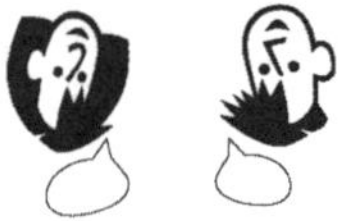

MISNOMER

noun (mihs noh muhr)

INCIPIENT

adj (ihn sihp ee uhnt)

synonym: curmudgeon

Scrooge was such a *misanthrope* that even the sight of children singing made him angry.

a person who hates or distrusts mankind

beginning to exist or appear; in an initial stage

> The *incipient* idea seemed brilliant, but they knew it needed much more development.

synonyms: developing, basic

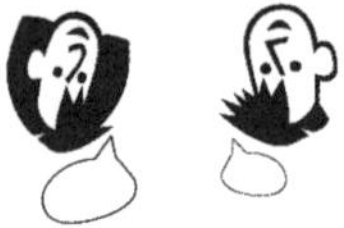

MISANTHROPE

noun (mihs uhn throhp)

INCORRIGIBLE

adj (ihn kohr ih juh buhl)

synonym: background

The *milieu* at the club wasn't one I was comfortable with, so I left right away.

the physical or social setting in which something occurs or develops, environment incapable of being corrected or changed; difficult to control or manage

> "You're *incorrigible*," yelled the frustrated mother to her son, in the middle of his third tantrum of the day.

synonyms: delinquent, unfixable

MILIEU

noun (mihl yoo̅)

INCREDULOUS

adj (ihn krehj uh luhs)

a small scale representation of a larger system

This department is in fact a *microcosm* of the entire corporation.

unwilling to accept what is said to be true, skeptical

The Lasky children were *incredulous* when their parents sat them down and told them the facts of life.

synonyms: doubtful, disbelieving

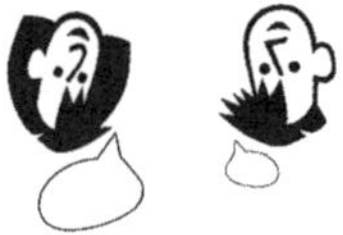

MICROCOSM

noun (mie kruh kahz uhm)

INDOMITABLE

adj (ihn dahm ih tuh buhl)

synonyms: melodious

She was so talented that her *mellifluous* flute playing transported me to another world.

having a smooth, rich flow

incapable of being conquered

Climbing Mount Everest would seem an *indomitable* task, but it has been done many times.

synonym: insurmountable

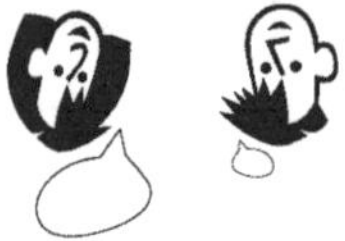

MELLIFLUOUS

adj (muh lihf loo uhs)

INGRATIATE

verb (ihn gray shee ayt)

obsession with great or grandiose performance

Many of the Roman emperors suffered from severe *megalomania.*

synonyms: egoism, self-centeredness

to gain favor with another by deliberate effort, to seek to please somebody so as to gain an advantage

> The new intern tried to *ingratiate* herself with the managers so that they might consider her for a future job.

synonyms: flatter, curry favor

MEGALOMANIA

noun (mehg uh loh may nee uh)

INHERENT

adj (ihn hehr ehnt)

sickeningly sentimental

The poet hoped to charm his girlfriend with his flowery poem, but its *mawkish* tone sickened her instead.

synonyms: maudlin

involved essential character of something, built-in, inborn

The class was dazzled by the experiment and as a result more likely to remember the *inherent* scientific principle.

synonym: intrinsic

MAWKISH

adj (maw kihsh)

an independent individual who does not go along with a group

The senator was a *maverick* who was willing to vote against his own party's position.

synonyms: nonconformist

INQUEST

noun (ihn kwehst)

an investigation, an inquiry

The police chief ordered an *inquest* to determine what went wrong.

MAVERICK

noun (maav rihk) (maav uh rihk)

INSENSATE

adj (ihn sehn sayt) (ihn sehn siht)

one who enjoys being subjected to pain or humiliation

Only a *masochist* would volunteer to take on this nightmarish project.

lacking sensibility and understanding, foolish

The shock of the accident left him *insensate*, but after some time, the numbness subsided and he was able to tell the officer what had happened.

synonyms: unfeeling, callous

MASOCHIST

noun (maas uhk ihst)

INSOLENT

adj (ihn suh luhnt)

artificial or stilted in character

The portrait is an example of the *mannered* style that was favored in that era.

synonyms: affected, unnatural

insultingly arrogant, overbearing

After having spoken with three *insolent* customer service representatives, Shelly was relieved when the fourth one sympathized with her complaint.

synonyms: offensive, rude

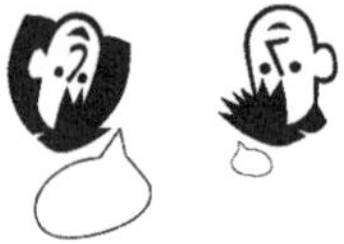

MANNERED

adj (maan uhrd)

INSULAR

adj (ihn suh luhr) (ihn syuh luhr)

synonyms: adaptable, pliable

The welder heated the metal before shaping it because the heat made it *malleable.*

easily influenced or shaped, capable of being altered by outside forces characteristic of an isolated people, especially having a narrow viewpoint

> It was a shock for Kendra to go from her small high school, with her *insular* group of friends, to a huge college with students from all over the country.

synonyms: provincial, narrow-minded

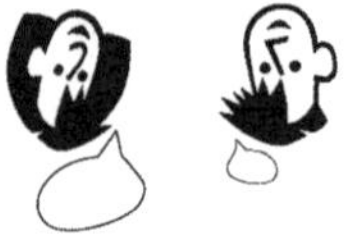

MALLEABLE

adj (maal ee uh buhl)

INSUPERABLE

adj (ihn <u>soo</u> puhr uh buhl)

wrongdoing or misconduct, especially by a public official

Not only was the deputy's *malfeasance* humiliating, it also spelled the end of his career.

synonyms: corruption, fraud

incapable of being surmounted or overcome

Insuperable as though our problems may seem, I'm confident we'll come out ahead.

synonym: unconquerable

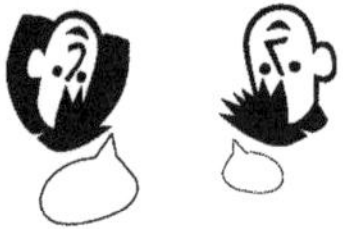

MALFEASANCE

noun (maal fee zuhns)

INTER

verb (ihn <u>tuhr</u>)

synonyms: malicious, hateful

The *malevolent* gossiper spread false rumors with frequency.

exhibiting ill will; wishing harm to others

to bury

After giving the masses one last chance to pay their respects, the leader's body was *interred*.

synonym: entomb

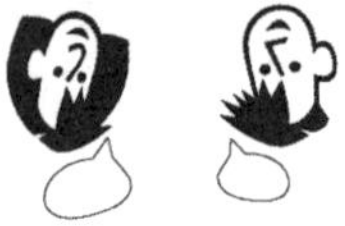

MALEVOLENT

adj (muh lehv uh luhnt)

INTERLOCUTOR

noun (ihn tuhr <u>lahk</u> yuh tuhr)

synonyms: damnation, commination

The frog prince looked for a princess to kiss him and put an end to the witch's malediction.

a curse, a wish of evil upon another

ones who takes part in conversation

> Though always the *interlocutor*, the professor actually preferred that his students guide the class discussion.

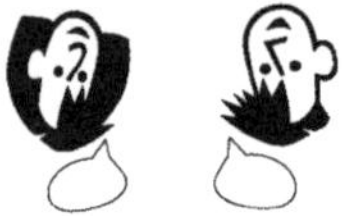

MALEDICTION

noun (mal ih dihk shun)

the accidental, often comical, use of a word which resembles the one intended, but has a different, often contradictory meaning

Everybody laughed at the *malapropism* when instead of saying "public broadcasting" the announcer said "public boredcasting."

synonym: misstatement

INTERNECINE

adj (ihn tuhr <u>nehs</u> een)

mutually destructive; equally devastating to both sides

Though it looked as though there was a victor, the *internecine* battle benefited no one.

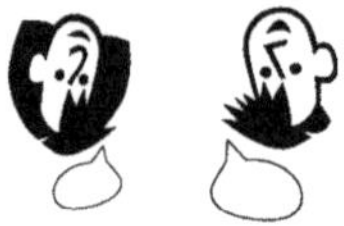

MALAPROPISM

noun (maal uh prahp ihz uhm)

INTERREGNUM

noun (ihn tuhr <u>rehg</u> nuhm)

a feeling of unease or depression

During his presidency, Jimmy Carter spoke of a "national *malaise*" and was subsequently criticized for being too negative.

synonyms: discomfort, unhappiness

a temporary halting of the usual operations of government or control

> The new king began his reign by restoring order that the lawless *interregnum* had destroyed.

synonyms: hiatus, interruption

MALAISE

noun (maa layz)

INTIMATION

noun (ihn tuh may shuhn)

synonym: cosmos

Some scientists focus on a particular aspect of space, while others study the entire *macrocosm* and how its parts relate to one another.

the whole universe; a large-scale reflection of a part of the great world a subtle and indirect hint

Abby chose to ignore Babu's *intimation* that she wasn't as good a swimmer as she claimed.

synonyms: suggestion, insinuation

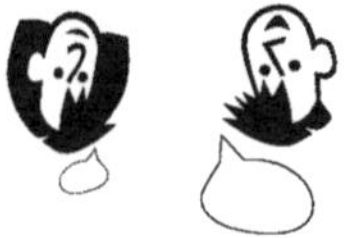

MACROCOSM

noun (maak roh kahz uhm)

INTRACTABLE

adj (ihn traak tuh buhl)

synonyms: ghastly, grim

Martin enjoyed *macabre* tales about werewolves and vampires.

having death as a subject; dwelling on the gruesome

not easily managed or manipulated

Intractable for hours, the wild horse eventually allowed the rider to mount.

synonyms: stubborn, unruly

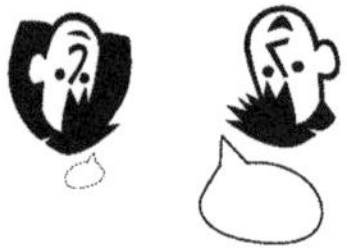

MACABRE

adj (muh kaa bruh) (muh kaa buhr)

INTRANSIGENT

adj (ihn traan suh juhnt) (ihn traan zuh juhnt)

talkative

She was naturally *loquacious*, which was always a challenge when she was in a library or movie theater.

synonym: chatty

uncompromising, refusing to abandon an extreme position

His *intransigent* positions on social issues cost him the election.

synonyms: obstinate, unyielding

LOQUACIOUS

adj (loh kway shuhs)

INTREPID

adj (ihn <u>trehp</u> ihd)

moving and bending with ease; marked by effortless grace

The dancer's *lithe* movements proved her to be a rising star in the ballet corps.

synonyms: flexible, limber

fearless, resolutely courageous

Despite freezing winds, the *intrepid* hiker completed his ascent.

synonym: brave

LITHE

adj (lieth)

INUNDATE

verb (<u>ihn</u> uhn dayt)

flexible, capable of being shaped

After years of doing so much yoga, the elderly man was remarkably *limber*.

synonyms: agile, nimble

to cover with a flood; to overwhelm as if with a flood

> The box office was *inundated* with requests for tickets to the award-winning play.

synonyms: swamp, drown

LIMBER

adj (lihm buhr)

INVETERATE

adj (ihn veht uhr iht)

a very small person or thing

Next to her Amazonian roommate, the girl appeared to be *lilliputian.*

synonyms: diminutive, small

firmly established, especially with respect to a habit or attitude

An *inveterate* risk-taker, Lori tried her luck at bungee-jumping.

synonyms: habitual, chronic

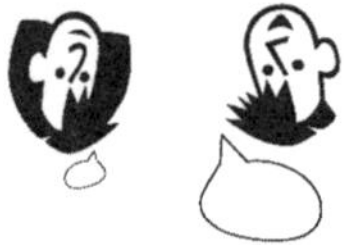

LILLIPUTIAN

noun (lihl ee pyoo shun)

IRASCIBLE

adj (ih raas uh buhl)

immoral; unrestrained by society

Religious citizens were outraged by the *licentious* exploits of the free-spirited artists living in town.

synonyms: wanton, lewd

easily angered, hot-tempered

> One of the most *irascible* barbarians of all time, Attila the Hun ravaged much of Europe during his time.

synonyms: irritable, crabby

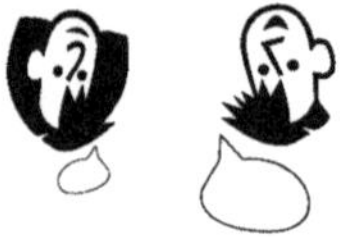

LICENTIOUS

adj (lei sehn shuhs)

IRONIC

adj (ie rahn ihk)

synonym: hedonist

The *libertine* took pleasure in gambling away his family's money.

a free thinker, usually used disparagingly; one without moral restraint poignantly contrary or incongruous to what was expected

It was *ironic* to learn that shy Wendy from high school grew up to be the loud-mouth host of the daily talk show.

LIBERTINE

noun (lihb uhr teen)

one who advocates individual rights and free will

The *libertarian* was always at odds with the conservatives.

IRREVERENT

adj (ih rehv uhr uhnt)

disrespectful in a gentle or humorous way

> Kevin's *irreverent* attitude toward the principal annoyed the teacher but amused the other children.

synonyms: cheeky, satiric

LIBERTARIAN

noun (lih buhr tehr ee uhn)

ITINERANT

adj (ie tihn uhr uhnt)

a dictionary; a stock of terms pertaining to a particular subject or vocabulary

The author coined the term Gen-X, which has since entered the *lexicon*.

synonyms: dictionary, vocabulary

wandering from place to place; unsettled

The *itinerant* tomcat came back to the Johansson homestead every two months.

synonyms: nomadic, vagrant

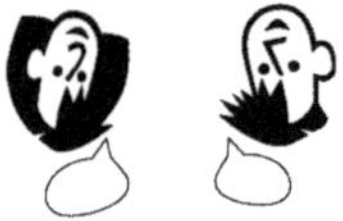

LEXICON

noun (lehk sih kahn)

JETTISON

verb (jeht ih zuhn) (jeht ih suhn)

synonyms: amusement, humor

The joke added needed *levity* to the otherwise serious meeting.

an inappropriate lack of seriousness, overly casual

to discard, to get rid of as unnecessary or encumbering

> The sinking ship *jettisoned* its cargo in a desperate attempt to reduce its weight.

synonyms: eject, dump

LEVITY

noun (leh vih tee)

JOCULAR

adj (<u>jahk</u> yuh luhr)

lewd, lustful

The school board censored the movie because of its portrayal of the *lecherous* criminal.

synonyms: lascivious, promiscuous

playful, humorous

The *jocular* old man entertained his grandchildren for hours.

synonyms: comical, amusing

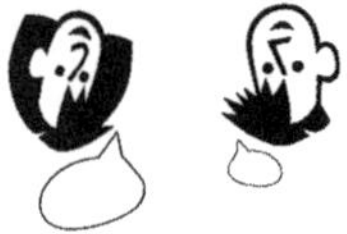

LECHEROUS

adj (lehch uh ruhs)

JUNTA

noun (<u>hoon</u> tuh) (<u>juhn</u> tuh)

synonyms: careless, imprecise

Because our delivery boy is *lax*, the newspaper often arrives sopping wet.

not rigid, loose; negligent

a small governing body, especially after a revolutionary seizure of power

> Only one member of the *junta* was satisfactory enough to be elected once the new government was established.

synonym: council

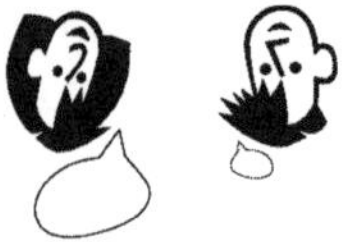

LAX

adj (laaks)

KISMET

noun (<u>kihz</u> meht) (<u>kihz</u> miht)

synonyms: commendable, admirable

Kristin's dedication is *laudable*, but she doesn't have the necessary skills to be a good paralegal.

deserving of praise

destiny, fate

When Eve found out that Garret also played the harmonica, she knew their meeting was *kismet*.

LAUDABLE

adj (law duh buhl)

LAMPOON

verb (laam <u>poon</u>)

generous giving (as of money) to others who may seem inferior

She'd always relied on her parent's *largess*, but after graduation, she had to get a job.

synonyms: generosity, benevolence

to ridicule with satire

> The mayor hated being *lampooned* by the press for his efforts to improve people's politeness.

synonyms: tease, mock, parody

LARGESS

noun (laar jehs)

SAT ROOT LIST

A, AN—not, without

AB, A—from, away, apart

AC, ACR—sharp, sour

AD, A—to, towards

ALI, ALTR—another

AM, AMI—love

AMBI, AMPHI—both

AMBL, AMBUL—walk

ANIM—mind, spirit, breath

ANN, ENN—year

ANTE, ANT—before

ANTHROP—human

ANTI, ANT—against, opposite

AUD—hear

AUTO—self

BELLI, BELL—war

BENE, BEN—good

BI—two

BIBLIO—book

BIO—life

BURS—money, purse

CAD, CAS, CID—happen, fall

CAP, CIP—head

CARN—flesh

CAP, CAPT, CEPT, CIP—take, hold, seize

CED, CESS—yield, go

CHROM—color

CHRON—time

CIDE—murder

CIRCUM—around

CLIN, CLIV—slope

CLUD, CLUS, CLAUS, CLOIS—shut, close

CO, COM, CON—with, together

COGN, GNO—know

CONTRA—against

CORP—body

COSMO, COSM—world

CRAC, CRAT—rule, power

CRED—trust, believe

CRESC, CRET—grow

CULP—blame, fault

CURR, CURS—run

DE—down, out, apart

DEC—ten, tenth

DEMO, DEM—people

DI, DIURN—day

DIA—across

DIC, DICT—speak

DIS, DIF, DI—not, apart, away
DOC, DOCT—teach
DOL—pain
DUC, DUCT—lead
EGO—self
EN, EM—in, into
ERR—wander
EU—well, good
EX, E—out, out of
FAC, FIC, FECT, FY, FEA—make, do
FAL, FALS—deceive
FERV—boil
FID—faith, trust
FLU, FLUX—flow
FORE—before
FRAG, FRAC—break
FUS—pour

GEN—birth, class, kin
GRAD, GRESS—step
GRAPH, GRAM—writing
GRAT—pleasing
GRAV, GRIEV—heavy
GREG—crowd, flock
HABIT, HIBIT—have, hold
HAP—by chance
HELIO, HELI—sun
HETERO—other
HOL—whole
HOMO—same
HOMO—man
HYDR—water
HYPER—too much, excess
HYPO—too little, under
IN, IG, IL, IM, IR—not

IN, IL, IM, IR—in, on, into
INTER—between, among
INTRA, INTR—within
IT, ITER—between, among
JECT, JET—throw
JOUR—day
JUD—judge
JUNCT, JUG—join
JUR—swear, law
LAT—side
LAV, LAU, LU—wash
LEG, LEC, LEX—read, speak
LEV—light
LIBER—free
LIG, LECT—choose, gather
LIG, LI, LY—bind
LING, LANG—tongue

LITER—letter
LITH—stone
LOQU, LOC, LOG—speech, thought
LUC, LUM—light
LUD, LUS—play
MACRO—great
MAG, MAJ, MAS, MAX—great
MAL—bad
MAN—hand
MAR—sea
MATER, MATR—mother
MEDI—middle
MEGA—great
MEM, MEN—remember
METER, METR, MENS—measure
MICRO—small
MIS—wrong, bad, hate
MIT, MISS—send
MOLL—soft
MON, MONIT—warn
MONO—one
MOR—custom, manner
MOR, MORT—dead
MORPH—shape
MOV, MOT, MOB, MOM—move
MUT—change
NAT, NASC—born
NAU, NAV—ship, sailor
NEG—not, deny
NEO—new
NIHIL—none, nothing
NOM, NYM—name
NOX, NIC, NEC, NOC—harm
NOV—new
NUMER—number
OB—against
OMNI—all
ONER—burden
OPER—work
PAC—peace
PALP—feel
PAN—all
PATER, PATR—father
PATH, PASS—feel, suffer
PEC—money
PED, POD—foot
PEL, PULS—drive
PEN—almost
PEND, PENS—hang
PER—through, by, for, throughout
PER—against, destruction

PERI—around
PET—seek, go towards
PHIL—love
PHOB—fear
PHON—sound
PLAC—calm, please
PON, POS—put, place
PORT—carry
POT—drink
POT—power
PRE—before
PRIM, PRI—first
PRO—ahead, forth
PROTO—first
PROX, PROP—near
PSEUDO—false
PYR—fire

QUAD, QUAR, QUAT—four
QUES, QUER, QUIS, QUIR—question
QUIE—quiet
QUINT, QUIN—five
RADI, RAMI—branch
RECT, REG—straight, rule
REG—king, rule
RETRO—backward
RID, RIS—laugh
ROG—ask
RUD—rough, crude
RUPT—break
SACR, SANCT—holy
SCRIB, SCRIPT, SCRIV—write
SE—apart, away
SEC, SECT, SEG—cut
SED, SID—sit

SEM—seed, sow
SEN—old
SENT, SENS—feel, think
SEQU, SECU—follow
SIM, SEM—similar, same
SIGN—mark, sign
SIN—curve
SOL—sun
SOL—alone
SOMN—sleep
SON—sound
SOPH—wisdom
SPEC, SPIC—see, look
SPER—hope
SPERS, SPAR—scatter
SPIR—breathe
STRICT, STRING—bind

STRUCT, STRU—build

SUB—under

SUMM—highest

SUPER, SUR—above

SURGE, SURRECT—rise

SYN, SYM—together

TACIT, TIC—silent

TACT, TAG, TANG—touch

TEN, TIN, TAIN—hold, twist

TEND, TENS, TENT—stretch

TERM—end

TERR—earth, land

TEST—witness

THE—god

THERM—heat

TIM—fear, frightened

TOP—place

TORT—twist

TORP—stiff, numb

TOX—poison

TRACT—draw

TRANS—across, over, through, beyond

TREM, TREP—shake

TURB—shake

UMBR—shadow

UNI, UN—one

URB—city

VAC—empty

VAL, VAIL—value, strength

VEN, VENT—come

VER—true

VERB—word

VERT, VERS—turn

VICT, VINC—conquer

VID, VIS—see

VIL—base, mean

VIV, VIT—life

VOC, VOK, VOW—call, voice

VOL—wish

VOLV, VOLUT—turn, roll

VOR—eat